I0827872

A Pilgrimage of Churches

SAINT JULIAN PRESS

POETRY

Praise for A PILGRIMAGE OF CHURCHES

A PILGRIMAGE OF CHURCHES will take the Reader on a powerful and transformative journey far into the heart of old and devotional America: to where the inspired and believing once established their vision of a true Jerusalem and of their Christ upon the coastal plains of Texas and up northward onto the plains of Kansas. This book is a gentle masterpiece of perception and human record, bringing back to life a world that has vanished from our Twenty-First Century culture. Like an ancient, illuminated manuscript this book will deliver lightness and conviction into your hands and eyes. Starbuck is a master of poetic tradition and diction, and his delivery of these prophetic songs – which vividly and precisely depict a forsaken time – returns us to those sacred grounds. About the author himself we can most certainly say that "his aim is true."

—Kevin McGrath, Harvard University

We all know the people of the Midwest have raised corn and crops forever, but they also raised churches, churches of many denominations, Methodist, Presbyterian, Catholic, AME, Baptist, Lutheran. On his midwestern and western pilgrimage, Ron Starbuck found both images and words that capture the holiness in both sacred and secular places in the middle of America.

In this collection, it almost feels as if Ron Starbuck has caught time sleeping as he delivers up images that seem pulled not just from the center of the country, but from the middle of the last century.

Time is stopped here and frozen, in the silvery light of these photographs. Ron Starbuck's poems, which invoke Biblical passages, cohere with these mesmerizing images to "pour out a radiance, A great reverence" for these far-flung and spiritual places.

Whether he is photographing tiny chapels and small-town clapboard churches or parking lots of John Deere tractors or plowed fields and pastures, these black-and-white images and liturgical-sounding poems evoke the same stark America as the WPA teams. Ron Starbuck is Walker Evans and James Agee rolled into one here, a new documentarian for a forgotten era of divine places.

—Elizabeth Cohen
The Family on Beartown Road: A Memoir of Love and Courage

A Pilgrimage of Churches

Sacred Spaces & Landscapes of America

Ron Starbuck

Saint Julian Press
Houston

Published by
SAINT JULIAN PRESS, Inc.
2053 Cortlandt, Suite 200
Houston, Texas 77008

www.saintjulianpress.com

Print-On-Demand - Second Edition – 202302
ISBN: 978-1-7330233-7-5
Library of Congress Control Number: 2021940319

Cover Design & Art Credit: Ron Starbuck
Cover Image: St. John Lutheran Church, Easton Township, Kansas
Author Photo Credit: Mary Beth Touchstone

PREFACE

Before my mother passed away, I made a promise to her and to myself. My promise was to stay connected with the farm community and countryside where she grew up. Northeastern Kansas is where her parents, along with her older brother and his wife, and many other relatives are laid to rest. Visiting this community required traveling 800 miles across the hills and prairies of Texas, Oklahoma, and most of Kansas from our home in Houston to Easton Township, Leavenworth County, Kansas.

Easton Township is the community where my maternal grandparents farmed and raised a family, as did their parents and grandparents before them. As children, my siblings and I spent many days on their homestead, which was like a second home, a place of safety and refuge. To this day, close cousins and relatives still attend St. John Lutheran Church and live in the area or within a single day's drive. This includes my cousins Rex Nelson Zabel and Della Kay Zabel-Sass, whose mother, Marlene Meinert-Zabel, was a bridesmaid at my mother's wedding, as well as my cousin Eileen Ruth Kern-Manning and her husband John Manning. Eileen and I had not seen one another since we were young children; they have helped me to explore our common genealogy. And helped me to connect with other relatives I never knew, including one living in Europe.

On this first journey back, I did not know that I would return several times to chronicle and cherish the landscape and country churches of Kansas. I was not there to begin a book or undertake a photo essay. I had journeyed there to grieve and to remember my mother in the place where her life began. I was there to keep my promise. It was only later, after some thought and reflection, when I became inspired to chronicle and reveal in photographs and poetry a remembrance and deeper discovery of my family's history and heritage. There I was able, with these images and words paired together in a poetic liturgy, to celebrate these sacred places of worship and the community life treasured across the Great Plains.

In the 1880s, my maternal family members arrived in the countryside northwest of Leavenworth, Kansas, where other families of German immigrants came to settle in America. My great-grandfather, Heinrich Wilhelm (William) Meinert, was born in Germany and came to America with his parents as a young child. His wife, my great-grandmother, Sophia Wilhelmine (Minnie) Moeller, immigrated with her parents when she was 23 years old. They were married in 1883 at St. John Lutheran. In those first fifteen years, they had eight children. My grandfather, born in 1894, was their sixth child. My grandmother was born in 1898. She and my grandfather married when he returned from France, after serving in World War I. They grew up together, attending the same school and church. This is where my grandparents wed in April 1920, right after the war and the Spanish Flu pandemic. Twenty-eight years later, after my father returned from serving in WWII and met my mother, my own parents were married in this same church in September 1948.

The story on my father's side is a similar one. After the American Civil War, my paternal great-grandfather, his four brothers and two sisters, first settled on the wide-open prairie in central Kansas. They arrived from Quaker communities in Richmond and Wayne County, Indiana. This is where their forebearers had settled from North Carolina in the Great Migration of Quakers after the War of 1812, moving westward, because they could not abide the practice of slavery. During the Civil War, the oldest of these five brothers, along with his father, served in the Union Army; the son training to become a physician. The Quaker faith practices pacifism and non-violence, so their military service cost them their family's place within the Quaker community. It also cost the father his life, when he died as a soldier from an unidentified illness. Following the conflict, the oldest son moved the family to central Kansas. His younger brother, my great-grandfather, Edward Macy Starbuck, eventually married a preacher's daughter, Rebecca Booker Gouldin. Her father, the Rev. Hiland Roper Gouldin, my second great-grandfather, was a Methodist Circuit Rider, who served several small Methodist churches in Lincoln County, Kansas. Rev. Gouldin also served in the Union Army during the Civil War and farmed a homestead north of Barnard, Kansas. On one of my road trips to the area, I decided to find his homestead by researching property records and discovered a third cousin I had never known.

To find my third-cousin, Rodney Gouldin, I drove down graded dirt roads, past fields and farms, and the cemetery where our shared relatives rest. In turning onto one of those country roads, I came across a farmhouse standing alone, and a mailbox with his last name painted in white on the side. I pulled off the road, and a man came out of the farmhouse wondering if I was a salesperson of sorts or a lost traveler. When I told him who I was and our family connection, his eyes lit up and he smiled. It was as if he was expecting someone from somewhere to happen by one day. Rodney Gouldin and I sat at his kitchen table to visit. "Look, at this," he exclaimed with excitement, showing me a wooden cane engraved with animals and scenes from the Bible that had once belonged to our second-great-grandfather and was carved by his son-in-law. He also brought out old newspaper clippings and obituaries and told me stories passed down from his parents and grandparents. Rodney's family lore recounts that my great-grandfather, Edward Macy Starbuck, whom they called Uncle Macy, helped to build the Barnard United Methodist Church that still serves the community today.

Rodney and I spent that afternoon together and drove to the nearby village of Simpson, Kansas where he bought me lunch at Trapper Joe's, a favored local café. I spent that night in Lincoln, the town where my father and his three siblings were born. The next day I drove back to Barnard and attended Sunday school and church services at the United Methodist Church, where I saw firsthand the workmanship of my great-grandfather. I stood at the communion rail and altar he once crafted. The church pianist, Kay Jackson, came up to me after the service and asked if I was related to someone from Vesper, the community where she grew up. It turned out that my aunt, Dorothy Jane Starbuck–Block, my father's elder sister, had taught her the piano. "There was a time I wanted to quit my piano lessons," she said, "but, my mother told me I'd have to inform Mrs. Block." They never had that conversation and I know why — my Aunt Dorothy was indomitable. Her children, my first-cousin Becky Block-Claus, whom I am as close to as my two sisters, and her brother, Royce Block, were also raised in Vesper. As children, we played together on their homestead and enjoyed meals at their family's table. Her father, my Uncle Richard, was always warmhearted and easy to be around. And yes, Becky learned the piano from her mother too, and loves it still. All these family and church connections interwove through my travels along with the endless prairie to inspire this book of poems. There are of course other cousins and relatives that I cannot all name. My father had a younger brother, Kenneth Clinton Starbuck, and another sister Kathleen June "Katy" Starbuck-Munson. This is a story and a family heritage my siblings and I share with all their children.

In the end, *A Pilgrimage of Churches* is one person's answer to the landscape of the Great Plains, flowing from Canada to the Coastal Plains of Texas, and the people who live there, who work the land, and who worship together in community on the Sabbath. These communities hold a rich heritage of faith and devotion that is an American story. It is a story we hold in common and share with many other Americans, whose families pioneered and settled the land generations before us. My desire is to tell it with a Quaker simplicity and sincerity that honors my own family's legacy. The poetry draws from a rich literary, artistic, and liturgical language, which reveals people of faith, and their intimate connection with the land that flourishes still, caring for and cultivating the American plains and prairies to help feed a Twenty-First Century world.

Ron Starbuck

Anno Domini Nostri Jesu Christi 2021

To the people and places of the Great Plains that have shaped this nation and hold its future.

And the end of all our exploring
Will be to arrive where we started
And know the place for the first time.
Through the unknown, unremembered gate
When the last of earth left to discover
Is that which was the beginning

—T. S. Eliot

CONTENTS

THE GLACIAL HILLS – GREAT PLAINS

PAGES 33 — 55

ST. JOHN LUTHERAN CHURCH – EASTON TOWNSHIP

FAMILY HOMESTEAD – EASTON TOWNSHIP

ST. PAUL'S EPISCOPAL CHURCH – LEAVENWORTH

BAKER UNIVERSITY – BALDWIN CITY

ST. MARY'S CATHOLIC CHURCH

ST. THOMAS EPISCOPAL CHURCH – HOLTON

GOFF UNITED METHODIST CHURCH

WETMORE UNITED METHODIST CHURCH

WETMORE FILLING STATION MUSEUM

THE FLINT HILLS – GREAT PLAINS

HOUSTON – COASTAL PLAINS

A Pilgrimage of Churches

A Pilgrimage of Churches

The Great Plains

Smoky Hills of Kansas

PSALM 116 *Dilexi, quoniam*

14 O LORD, I am your servant;
I am your servant and the child of your handmaid;
you have freed me from my bonds.

15 I will offer you the sacrifice of thanksgiving
and call upon the Name of the LORD.

16 I will fulfill my vows to the LORD
in the presence of all his people,

17 In the courts of the LORD'S house,
in the midst of you, O Jerusalem.
Hallelujah!

IN THIS HOLY HOUSE – SHEKHINAH

United Methodist Church – Beverly, Kansas

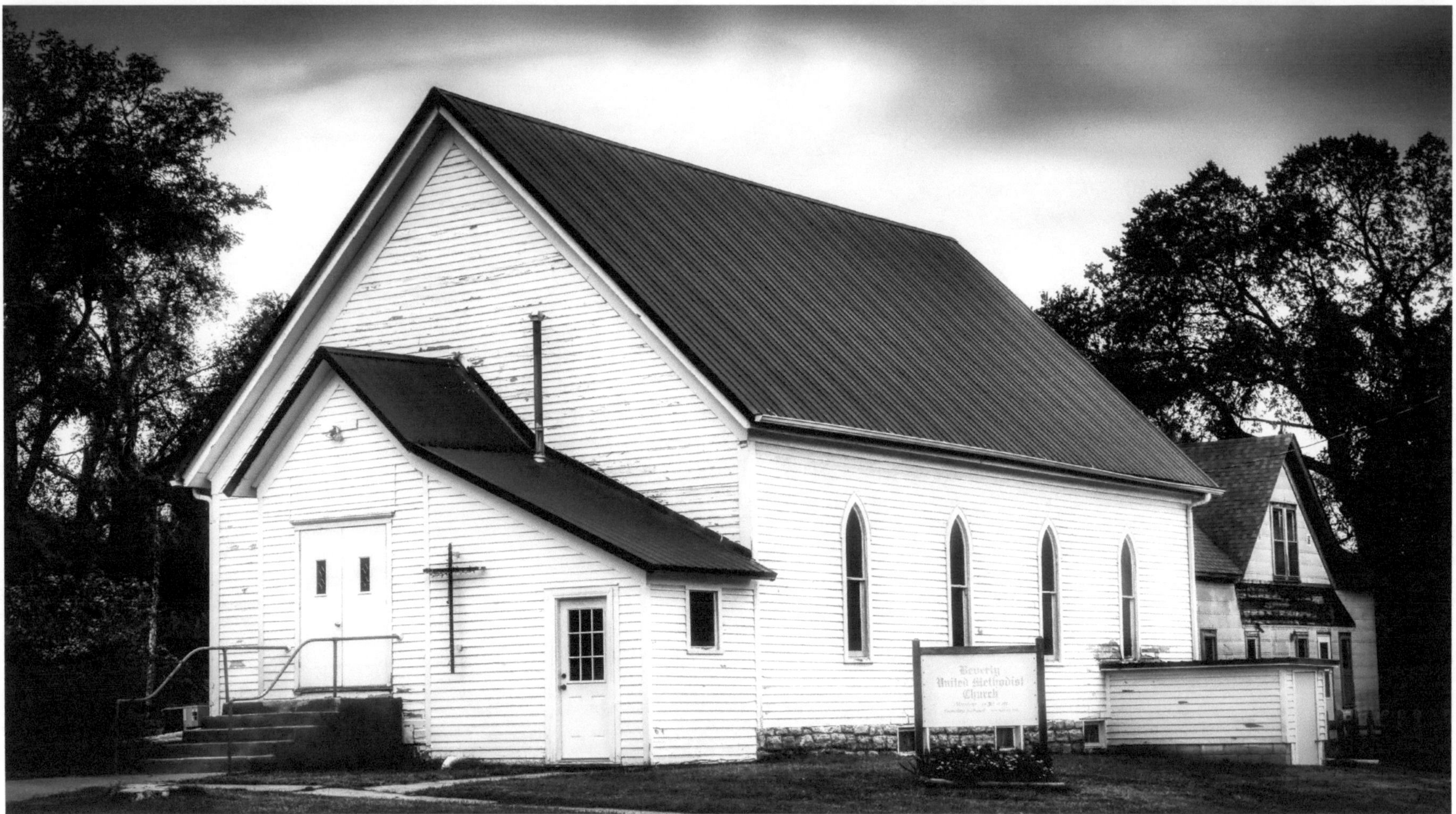

IN THIS HOLY HOUSE - SHEKHINAH

PSALM 51 Miserere mei, Deus
11 Create in me a clean heart, O God;
and renew a right spirit within me.
12 Cast me not away from thy presence;
and take not thy holy spirit from me.

We must imagine, beyond
All our visions — in every
Holy House of God

An indwelling, a settling
Of the *Holy Spirit* — shekhinah
An abundance of light

That rises up
As the last darkness
Passes over humankind

And transforms all things
Pouring out a radiance
A great reverence

A divine presence dwelling
Within all flesh — as humanity's
Sons and daughters prophesy

In a reconciliation and
Redemption within the world
In a name given and exalted

Above every name in heaven
Upon and under the earth
Confessed on every tongue

So that we might too
Become servants emptied
Of all presumptions and desires

VESPER PRESBYTERIAN CHURCH

Vesper, Lincoln County, Kansas

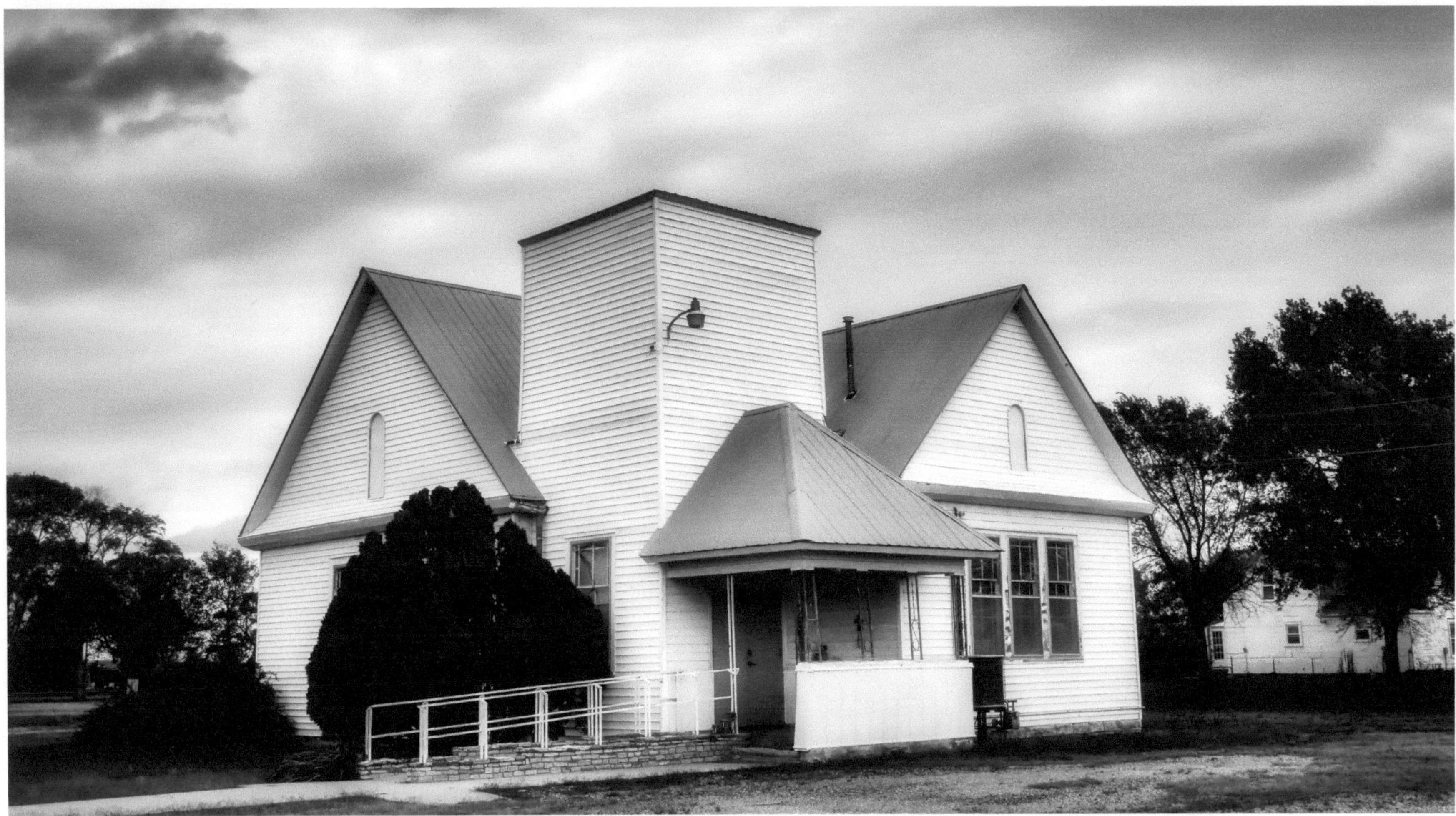

VESPER PRESBYTERIAN CHURCH

1 CORINTHIANS 13 – (NRSV) 12 For now we see in a mirror, dimly, but then we will see face to face. Now I know only in part; then I will know fully, even as I have been fully known.

John Knox never imagined
How future Presbyterians would
One day arrive in the New World
To steward and till the land
Where children and grandchildren
And their offspring would grow
As high and resilient as wheat
Planted under a winter sun
Bright with a promise of America
By their forbearers from distant
And troubled nations without
Peace or plenty or choice
Raising when they first arrived
White wooden churches
Across a sea of prairie grassland
Blown clean by God's breath
Across fields fertile in mercy
And what was to be a renewing
And abundant generosity
Where they could see both
Near and far past all doubt
In a grander hope aspiring
To the utmost curving heaven
Where at night a perfect light
Would gather and bend inward
As stars congregate to observe
Within a hushed stillness
Answering with a mighty
Chorus from which creation
Bravely expands even now
Reflecting a celestial splendor
Of this concealed mystery
Imperceptible to humankind
Wondering if we will
Ever know and be known
By such an intimate force
Believing in this longing
An aspiration of moral lives
Cultivating the countryside
As another generation
Adopts a heritage of faith
Ascending from blessed *terra*
Receiving from John Knox all
These blessings made with prayer

ABANDONED SCHOOLHOUSE & SOYBEAN FIELD

Lincoln County, Kansas

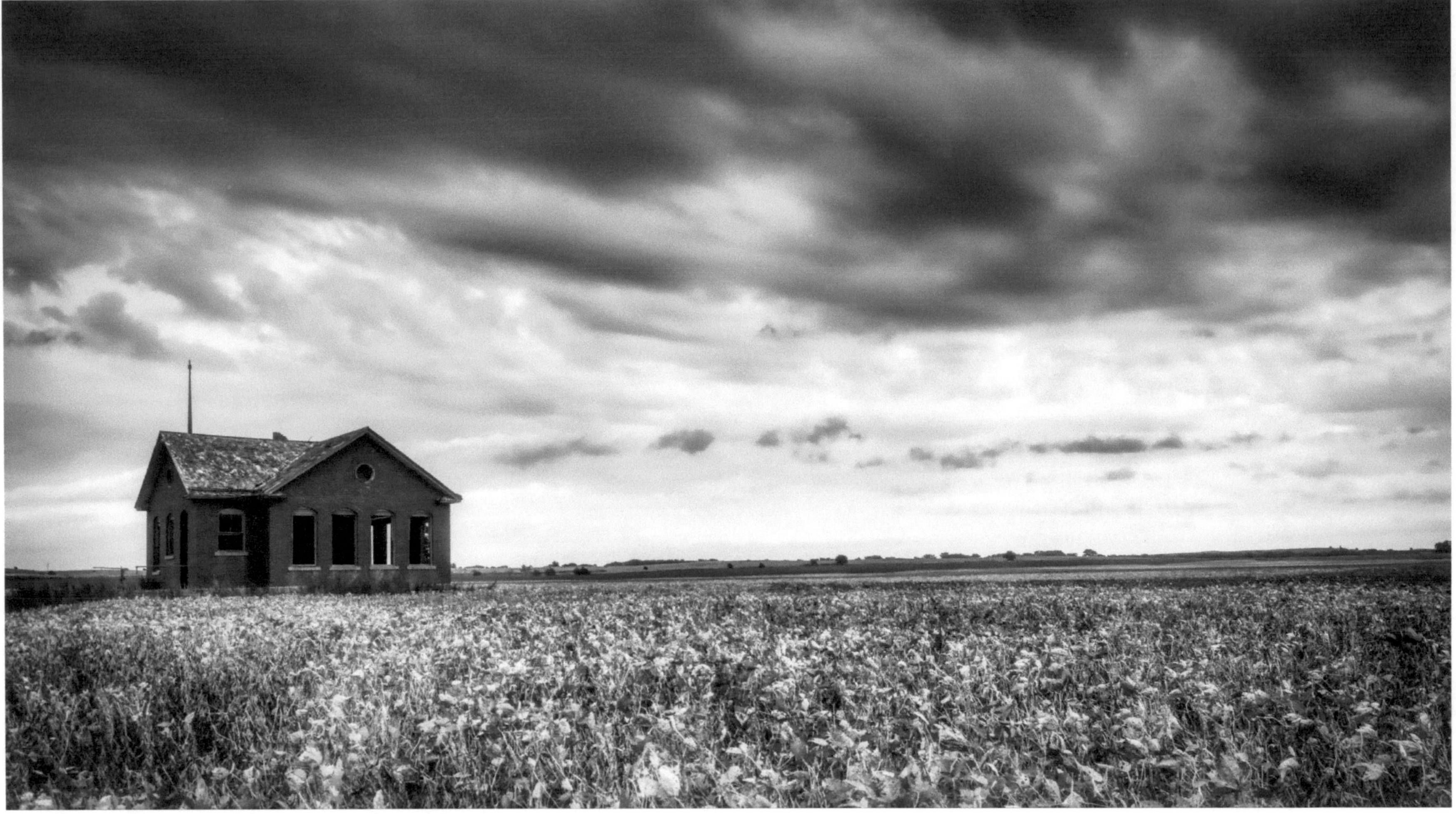

VESPER PRESBYTERIAN CHURCH

PSALM 95 Venite, exultemus

6 Come, let us bow down, and bend the knee,
and kneel before the Lord our Maker.
7 For he is our God,
and we are the people of his pasture and the sheep of his hand.
Oh, that today you would hearken to his voice!

Nor could John Knox imagine
How my first cousin's family
And all the circling farm families
Gathered each Sunday
To sit in their chosen pews
The family conversations
And talk of the week's labor
The crops to plant in spring
And those to harvest in fall
Although winter wheat was cut
In early summer long before
The corn grew high in autumn
Fields brushed with tawny colors
Pumpkin dreams grown plush
From summer sun and rain
The children's delightful school days
How they employed every nook
And cranny found to teach
Each single grade Sunday school
Honored stories from the Bible
Learned by memory and recited
How the Hebrews wandered
In the desert for forty years
Led by Joshua and Caleb
To the Promised Land
Filled with milk and honey
Or how Sunday evening
Became a 'Singspiration'
As they called it then
A celebration of hymns
Her mother my aunt
Playing the piano
Each service – her father
Sitting alone with the kids
And nurtured as a community
All the children together
As only a village parish
May do each generation
And Holy Communion
Offered so rarely it became
A sacrament treasured
Once each quarter
Binding them together
As a people of faith

GENERATIONS

Denmark Lutheran Church – Denmark, Kansas

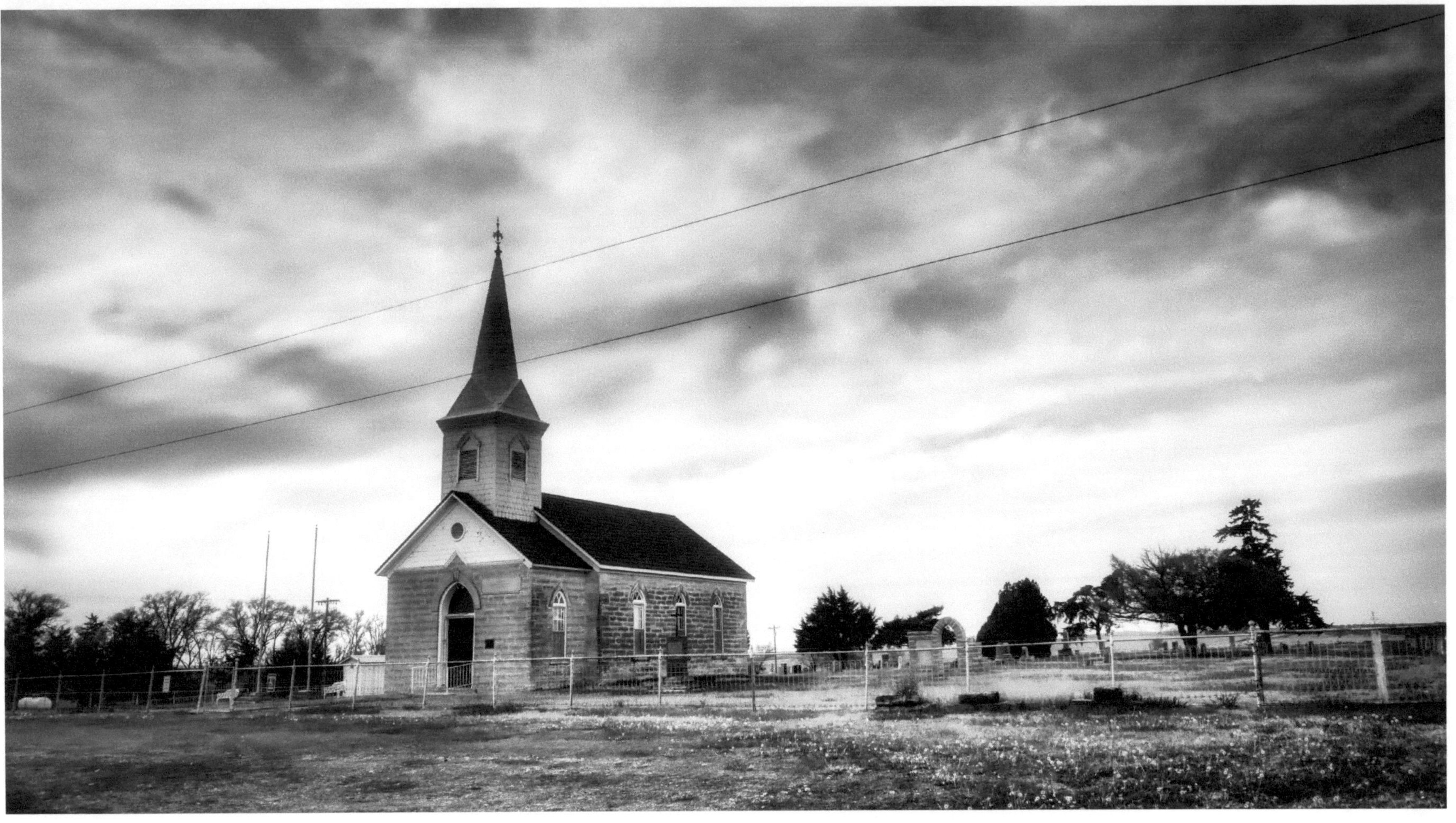

GENERATIONS

LUKE 1– (AKJV)

26 And in the sixth month the angel Gabriel was sent from God unto a city of Galilee,
named Nazareth, 27 to a virgin espoused to a man whose name was Joseph, of the house
of David; and the virgin's name was Mary. 28 And the angel came in unto her, and said,
Hail, thou that art highly favoured, the Lord is with thee: blessed art thou among women.

Every year during Advent
This blessed community
Gathers together to hold
A special celebration
Festival of the Nativities
To declare the mysteries
From ancient times
To honor the Christ child
The lessons of our childhood
Remain with us all our lives
Coming to dwell within us
In a blessed assurance of faith
Flowing in and with and through
Our collective minds
In the lives of many people
Across many generations
This is what I imagine Christ
Had in mind for the universal church
The stories and parables we tell
And teach each generation
Sanctified within us become
Living metaphors of poetic
Verse that touches the deepest
Fathoms of our soul and being
Manna and grain from heaven
Words spoken in the sacred tongue
Of angels and archangels
And the *Holy Spirit* who awakens
Within an indwelling so that mere
Mortals may eat the bread of angels
In a transformation we've always known
Giving birth to our own Nativity
In a commemoration we celebrate
Each year at Christmastide

GOD OF ABRAHAM

United Methodist Church – Waldo, Kansas

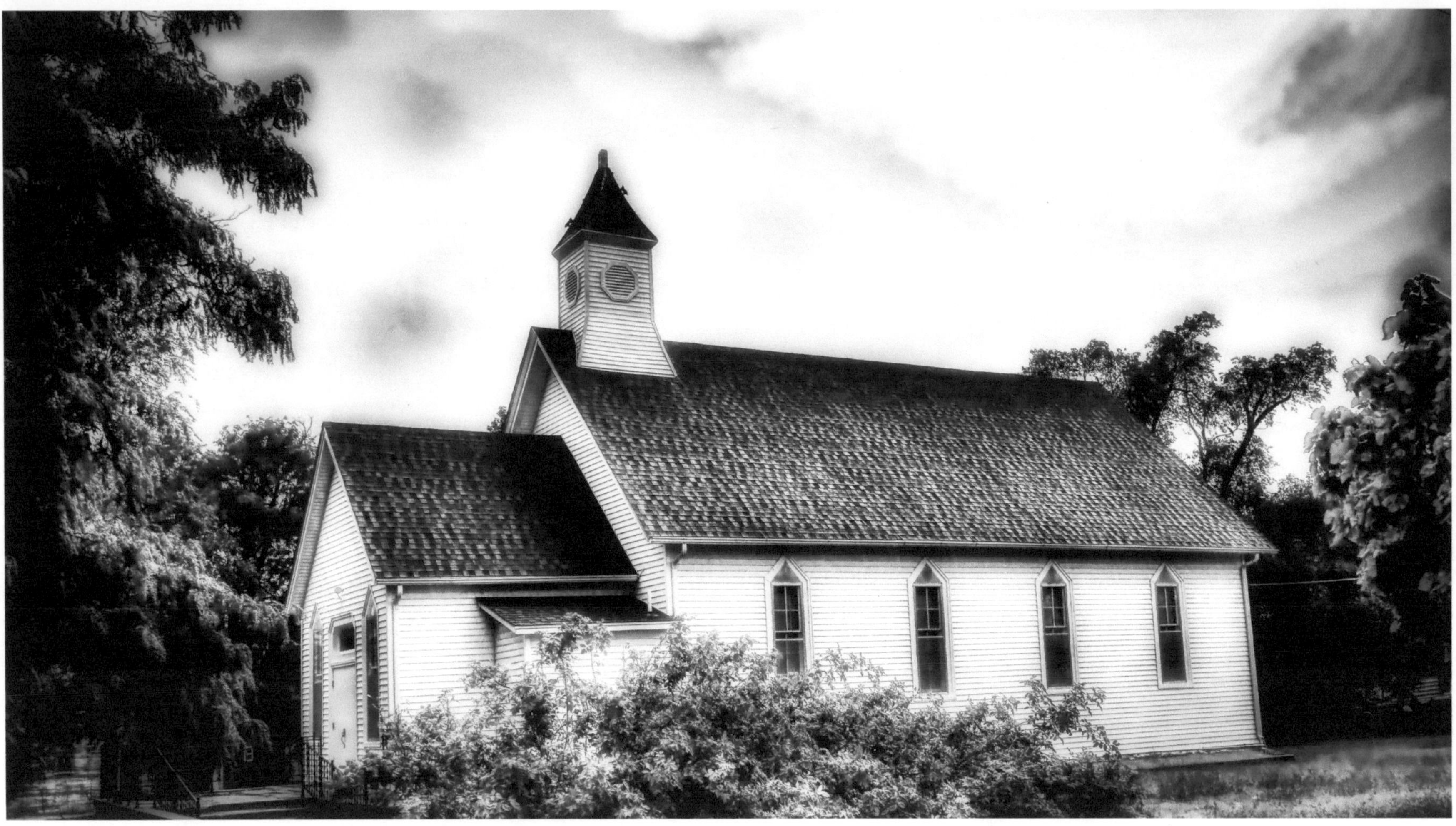

GOD OF ABRAHAM

PSALM 84 Quam Dilecta!

2 The sparrow has found her a house
and the swallow a nest where she may lay her young;
by the side of your altars, O Lord of hosts,
my King and my God.
3 Happy are they who dwell in your house!
they will always be praising you.

Here is a humble house built
With human hands and hallowed
Where the God of Abraham, Isaac
And Jacob dwells forevermore

How lovely is thy dwelling place
Thou Lord of Hosts
Our souls long for thee – we cry
Out to the living Lord

Blessed are those who dwell together
In this consecrated sanctuary
Revealed to us as thy presence
Resting here within

In this sacred home of worship
This small church and sanctuary
We praise thee – who welcomes
Us to thy courts with love

In this fulfillment of thy promise
And purpose going back to Abraham
Where we come to know and
Are forever known by thee

This is why we celebrate together
Within this Holy House of God
An everlasting undying love
The birth of innocence

United Methodist Church – Natoma, Kansas

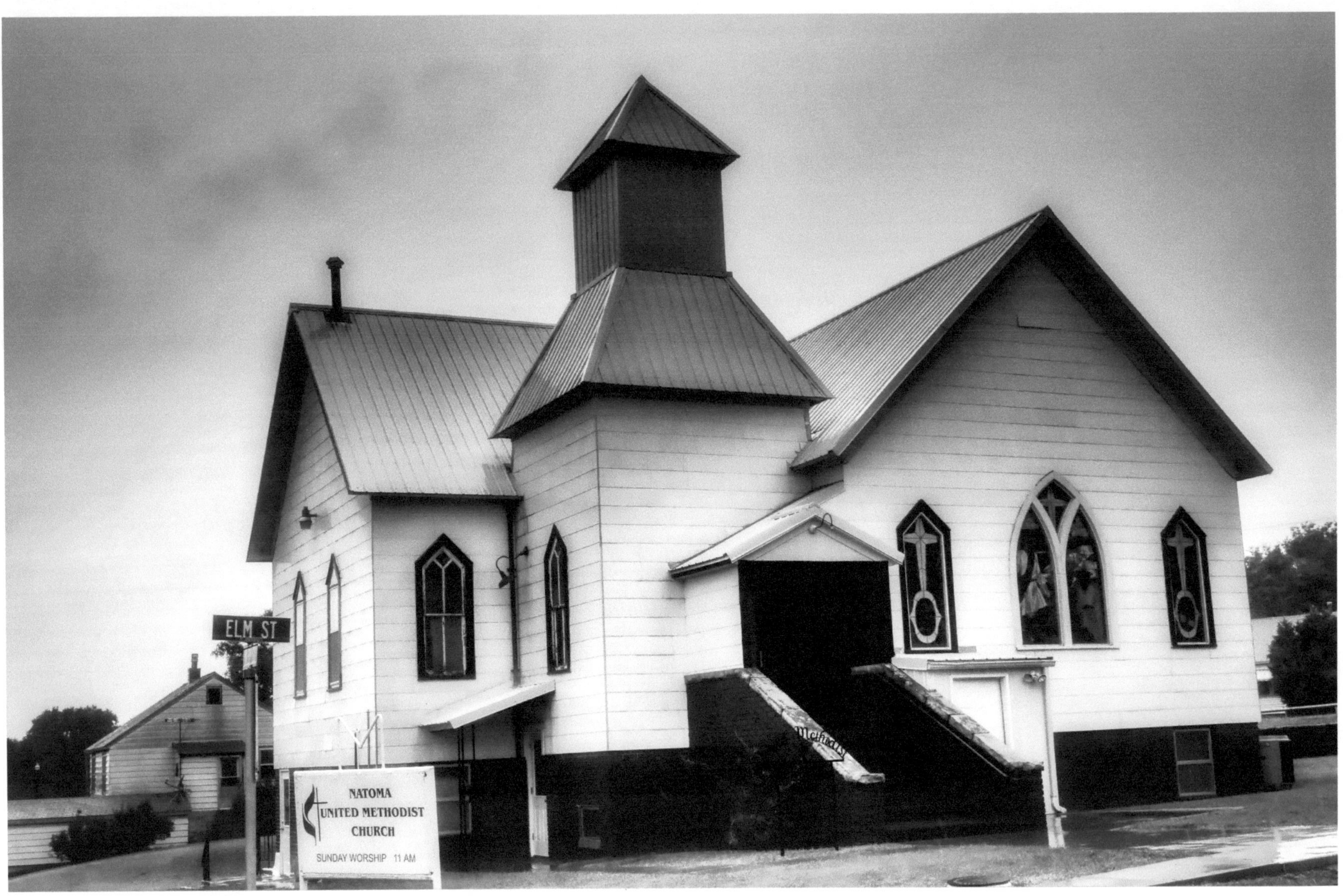

PARADISE CREEK

PSALM 1 *Beátus vir, qui non abiit*

3 They are like trees planted by streams of water,
bearing fruit in due season, with leaves that do not wither;
everything they do shall prosper.

Once the Tallgrass Prairie grew high
Along the banks of Paradise Creek
Where the prairie waters offer
A symphony of flowing songs
Running easy across wise stones
That remember each rainfall
Held gently and sonorous through
Lingering ages of earth and wind
Where cottonwoods and willow
Composed dreams from the music
Arising in a chorus of new psalms
Blessed by a landscape rich and
Abundant with Whitetail Deer
Beaver antelope elk bison coyote
Roaming across windblown savannahs
Where an indigenous people
The Cheyenne and Arapaho
The Comanche and Kiowa
Once hunted among hills and valleys
Throughout the Southern Plains
For generations before immigrant
Feet seeking their own liberation
Travelled westward across America
Bringing Methodist Presbyterian
Catholic and Lutheran kin
From afar to settle in this corner
Of the Smoky Hills – arriving
With the railway in the 1880s
They named Natoma Kansas
After a Native American worker
Whose name means *New–Born*
And so — an agricultural
Society of farms and ranches
Was given birth and rose beside
Stream and creek flowing into
The Saline and Smoky Hill Rivers
Sculpting the vales and leas in
Fertile tones of laurel umber and sienna
To merge with the Solomon and Republican
Rivers enthralled to the *Kaw* River
In a fluid current down to the *Big Muddy*
Then to the vast Mississippi River
Mother to a nation of builders
Curving south toward Baton Rouge
New Orleans and an ocean
Of blue promises and mirrored stars

SOLOMON RIVER WATERFALL
Minneapolis, Kansas

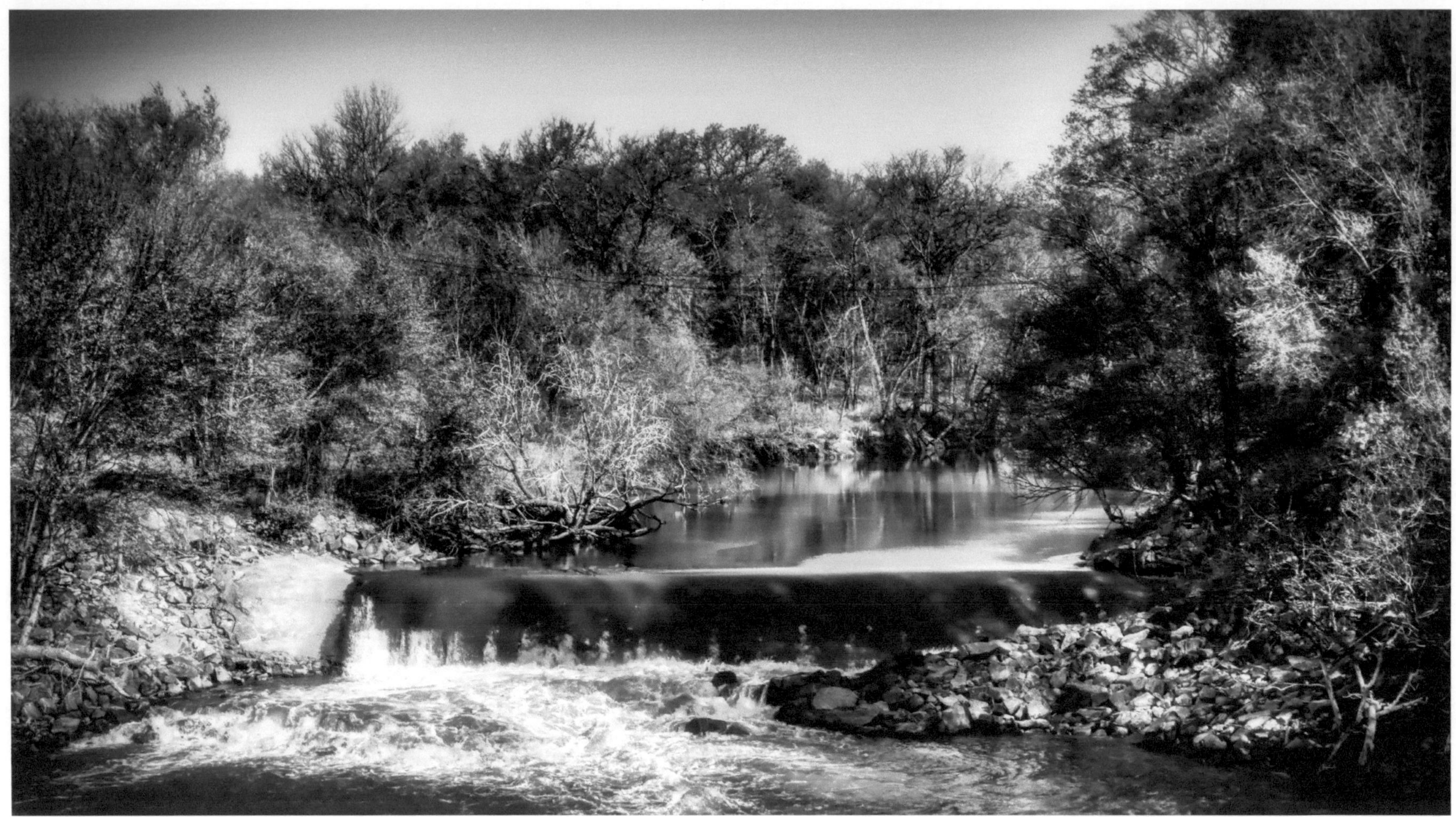

SOLOMON RIVER WATERFALL

PSALM 126 In convertendo
5 Restore our fortunes, O Lord,
like the watercourses of the Negev.
6 Those who sowed with tears
will reap with songs of joy.

Before the prairie rains
First fell to transform
Stream and brook to running
Rivers and deep waterfalls
Before the curious wind
Caressed the Tallgrass Prairie
Before each hill and valley
Was sculpted in artistic curves
No human hand could rival
Where God looked upon
This tender sacred land
Gathering light and shadow
Together to cast forth
Bright chiaroscuro dreams
As heirs and caring stewards
We could little imagine
Earth's untouched innocence
The grace filled splendor
Where fluid landscapes drift

Amid windblown waves of Bluestem
Pastures flowing over prairie
Rise and dale where bison herds
Tread tall grasses gently to forage
And renew the soil each solstice
Healing the timeworn earth
Gathering into one body
Each spring in a synchronous
Time which brings forth
Newborn calves revered
Each season in thanksgiving
In devotion and remembrance
A holy prayer celebrating
Creation and wonder
To unveil all we observe
In a consciousness of faith
Now fully revealed
As the mirrored image
Of God's immanence

FIRST UNITED METHODIST CHURCH
Barnard, Kansas

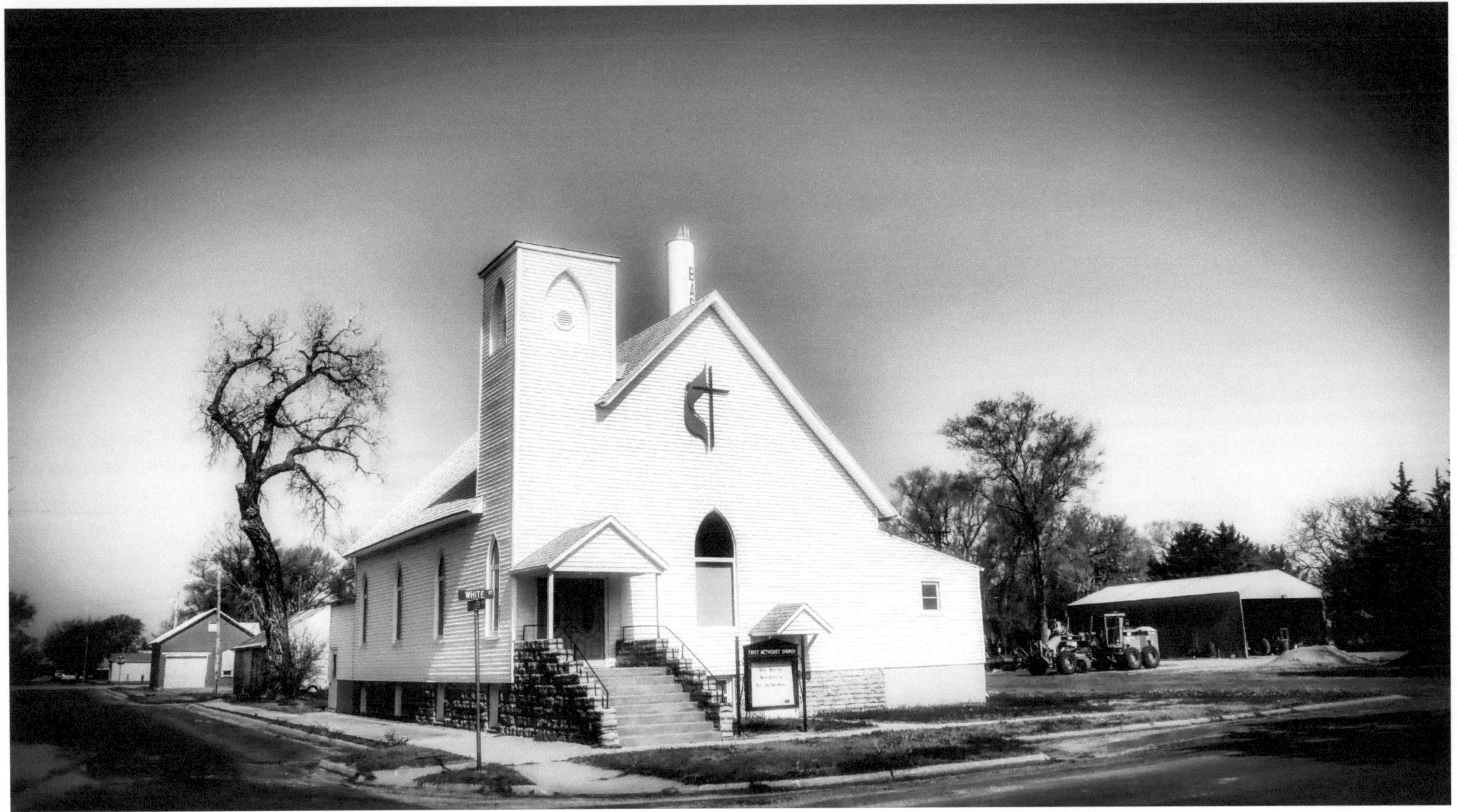

NEW JERUSALEM

PSALM 122 Lætatus sum

1 I was glad when they said to me,
"Let us go to the house of the Lord."
2 Now our feet are standing
within your gates, O Jerusalem.
3 Jerusalem is built as a city
that is at unity with itself

The people and community
Who once built this church
Never questioned why
This was their New Jerusalem
John Winthrop's – City Upon a Hill
To become in time
A light of the world
They knew what was needed
A sacred place to gather
Together as one people
In worship and celebration
In the sacraments of faith
Known so intimately
In Holy Baptism at birth
In Penitent Reconciliation
In Holy Eucharist and Communion
In Confirmation and Affirmation
Honored in liturgical verses
In an everlasting language

There is one Body and one Spirit
There is one hope in God's call to us
One Lord, one Faith, one Baptism
One God and Father of all
Renewing Baptismal vows
In Celebration and Blessing of Marriage
In Ministration to the Sick
In Healing and at Time of Death
In the Burial of the Dead
In Ordinations of Bishops Clergy
Elders Priests and Deacons
In Celebration of New Ministries
In Consecration of Church or Chapel
In Godly Play for Child and Youth
In the everyday life and prayer
That sustains us all and the world
In faith filled traditions arising
Since the time of Christ's two
Greatest commandments

FIRST UNITED METHODIST CHURCH

Barnard, Kansas

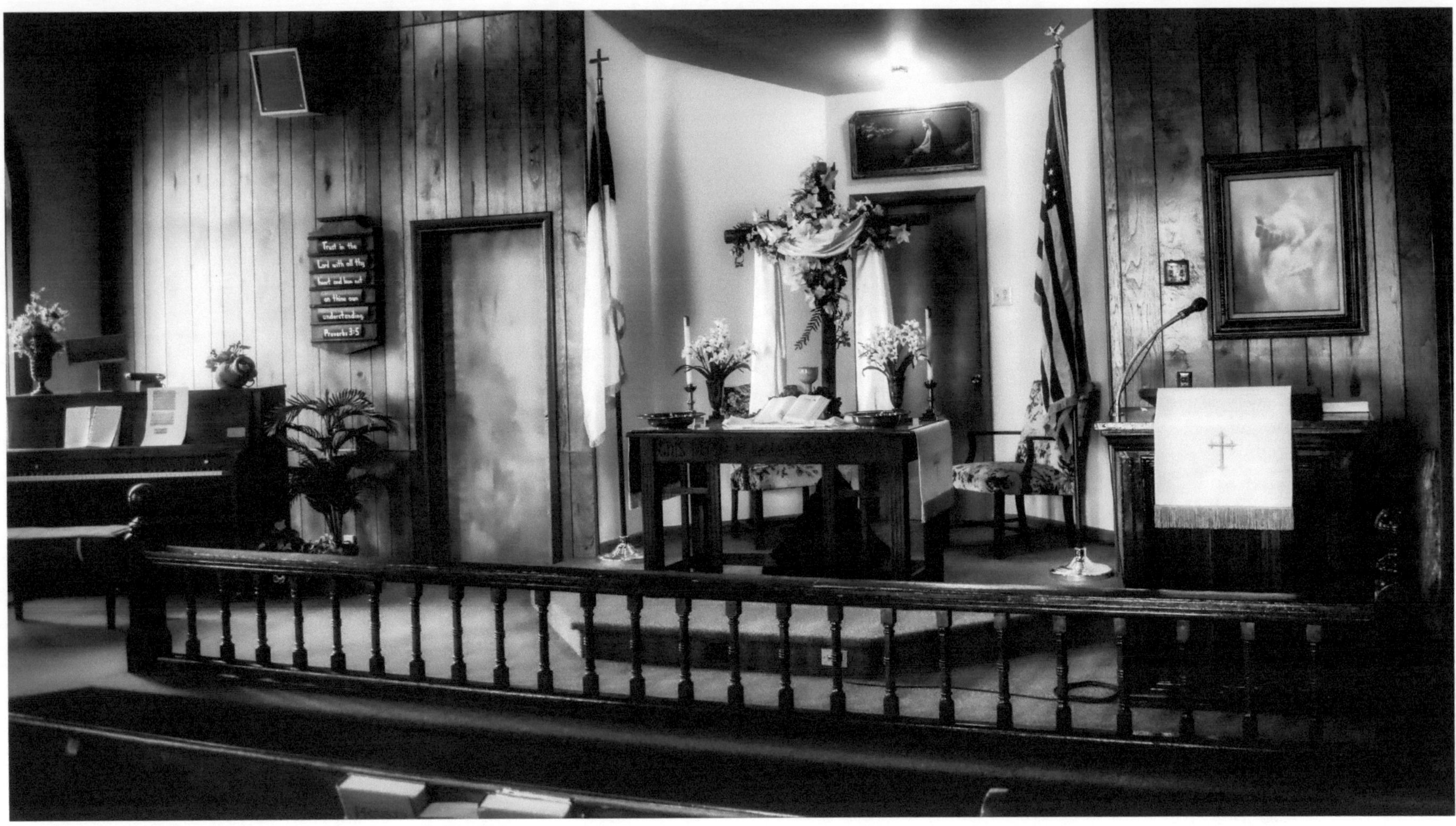

HOLY ALTAR

PSALM 26 Judica me, Domine

6 I will wash my hands in innocence, O Lord,
that I may go in procession round your altar,
7 Singing aloud a song of thanksgiving
and recounting all your wonderful deeds.
8 Lord, I love the house in which you dwell
and the place where your glory abides.

In this sacred place O Lord
A place of prayer and humble access
May we find worthy reception
Upon this your Holy Altar
Where you take no delight
Or desire in sacrifices
And burnt offerings
Here we may only offer
To you O Lord ourselves
Our broken hearts
And spirits as they are now
In this new day
In each new day
We live to serve thee
As the day arises

In the greater glory
Of the risen Christ
Within us each
Our many sorrows
Are without measure
And unfathomable
A hollowed contriteness
Marked by an inability
To see beyond ourselves
Make clean our hearts
O Lord and Renew
A Right Spirit within us
Open our lips O Lord
And we will sing
Forth thy praises

UNION PACIFIC TRAIN DEPOT

Simpson, Kansas

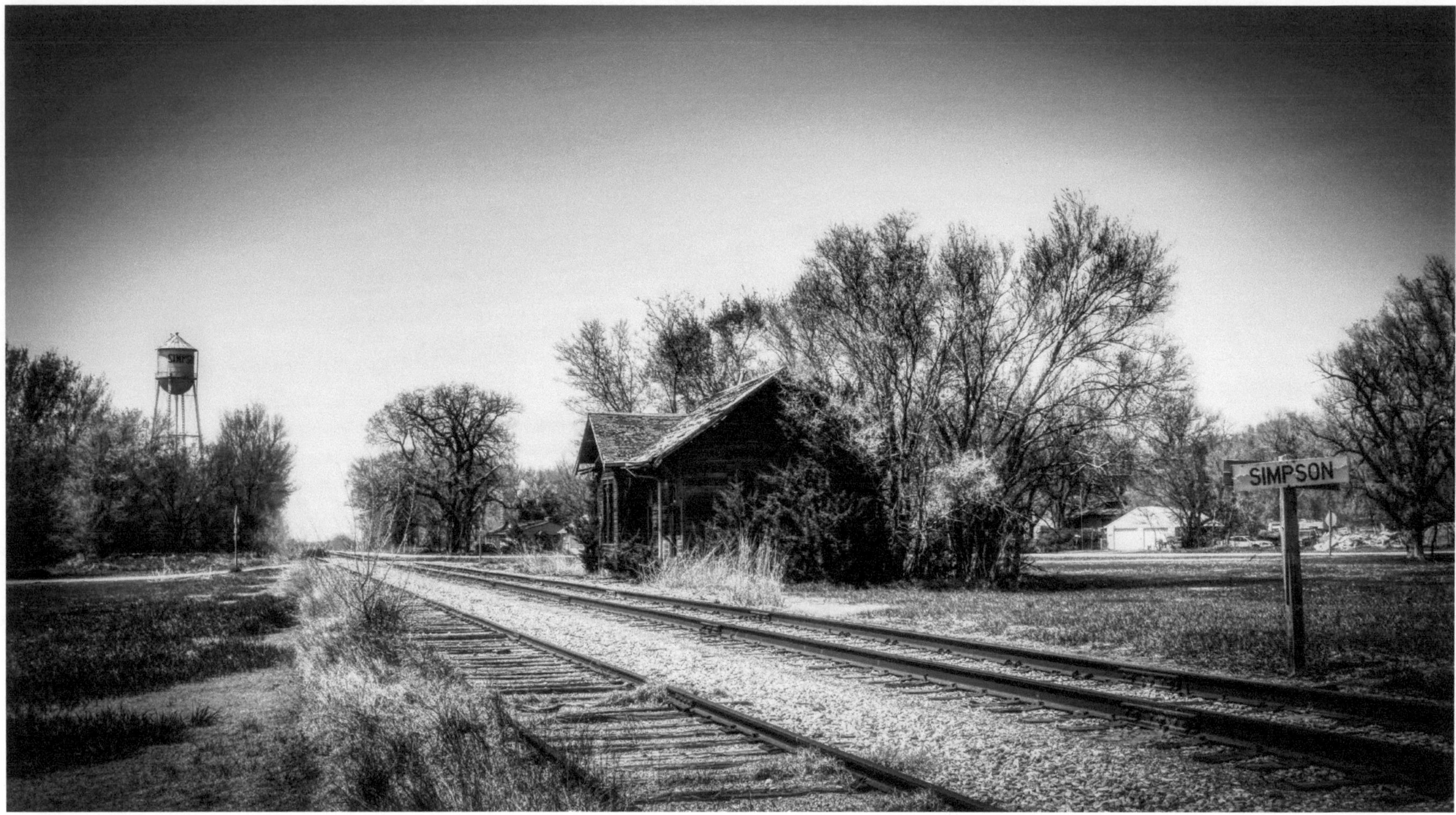

UNION PACIFIC TRAIN DEPOT

PSALM 139 Domine, probasti

1 Lord, you have searched me out and known me;
you know my sitting down and my rising up;
you discern my thoughts from afar.
2 You trace my journeys and my resting-places
and are acquainted with all my ways.

Long before the many
Abandoned train stations
And small-town depots
With endlessly moving tracks
Fell into ruin to become
A fading remembrance
When the land belonged
To no one in particular
Even indigenous tribes
That appeared and left
With the blowing wind
Never leaving a trace
As each season passed
And the bison herds
Migrated and gathered
Crossing a prairie sea
From one place or another
Long before and even

After pioneer people travelled
Past the plains and prairies
Still seen and known today
To settle and farm the land
Long before the railroad
Lines were built following
Riparian forest and woodland
Beside clear running streams
Where Cottonwood
Black Willow Ash Elm
And Box Elder grew lush
In spring and summer
Then shed their painted leaves
In autumn's fading light
A rarer consciousness blessed
The land and holds it still today
In vibrant beauty and holiness
In a timeless memory

AFRICAN METHODIST EPISCOPAL CHURCH

Nicodemus, Kansas – Nicodemus National Historic Site

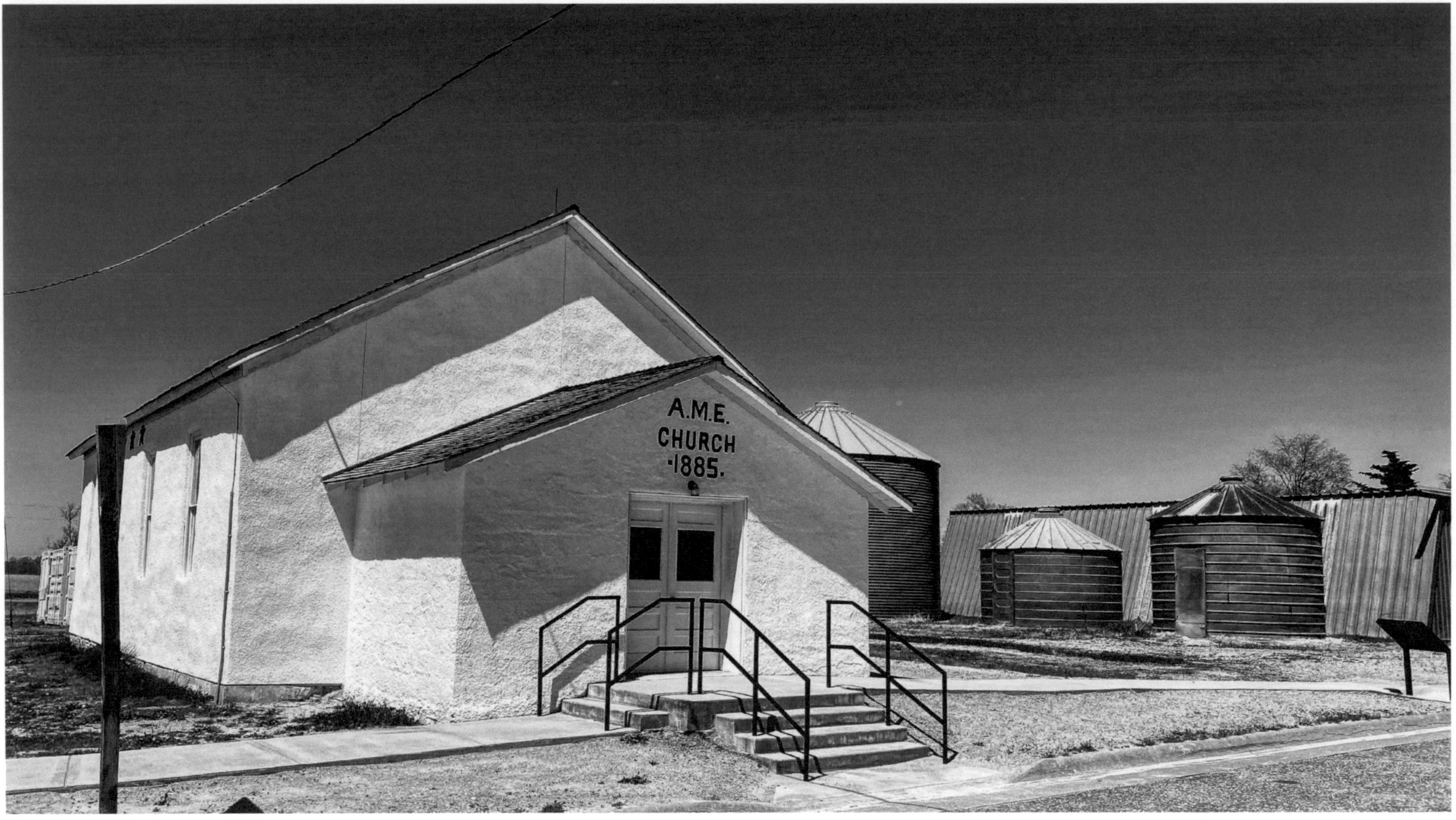

NICODEMUS RISES

JOHN 3 – (NRSV)

5 Jesus answered, "Very truly, I tell you, no one can enter the kingdom of God without being born of water and Spirit. 6 What is born of the flesh is flesh, and what is born of the Spirit is spirit."

Absalom Jones and Richard Allen
Ordained as Episcopal
And Methodist clergy
Could little imagine how one day
Nicodemus Kansas would rise
From the Great Plains of America
Among the Smoky Hills
Where wooded streams flow
Ceaselessly downward to the
South Fork Solomon River
Meandering along meadow and valley
Lush with green prairie grasslands
Amid chalk-colored hills airy-skies
Abundant wildlife — deer turkey quail
Pheasant and vibrant wildflowers
Wading in the troubled waters of Jordan
Where Moses led the Israelites
A new community of believers
Who sought a freedom
And society never known before
Refugees from Southern States
Newly coined as American citizens
Seeking the Promised Land
In fertile fields and countryside
In an exodus by the thousands
To claim acres and homesteads
Their story is an immigrant one
A story of how they endured
Dauntless and hope filled
With resilience and resistance
They took up residence alone
Among tentative neighbors
To create a new history
Standing together as one
People — finding a renewed
Unity and freedom in its name
As their children stood tall
And still stand high today
Far from Egypt's land
Nicodemus ever rises
Born again and again
In water and *Spirit*

ST. JOSEPH CATHOLIC CHURCH

Damar, Kansas

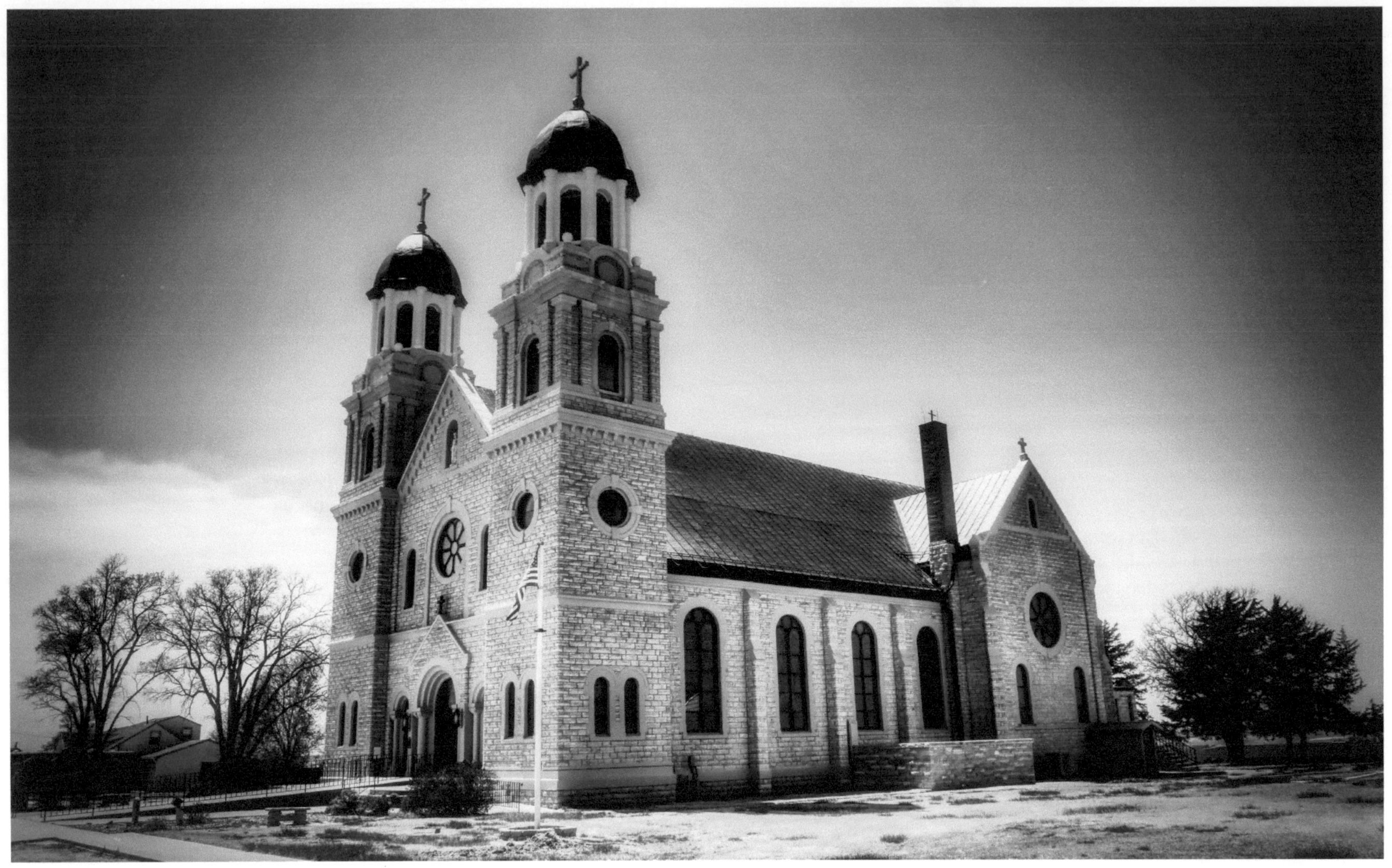

ST. JOSEPH CATHOLIC CHURCH
Damar, Kansas

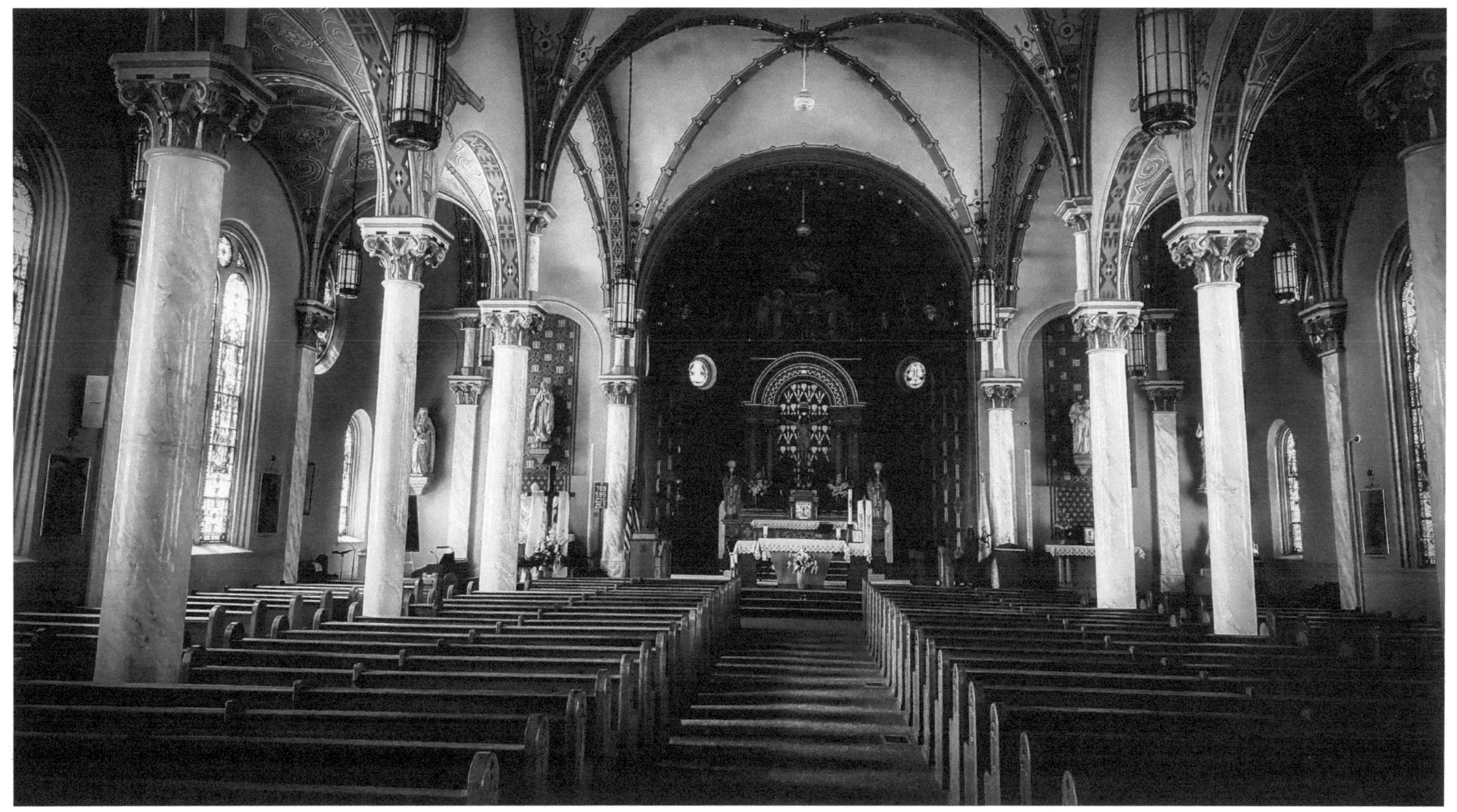

AGRA UNITED METHODIST CHURCH

Agra, Kansas

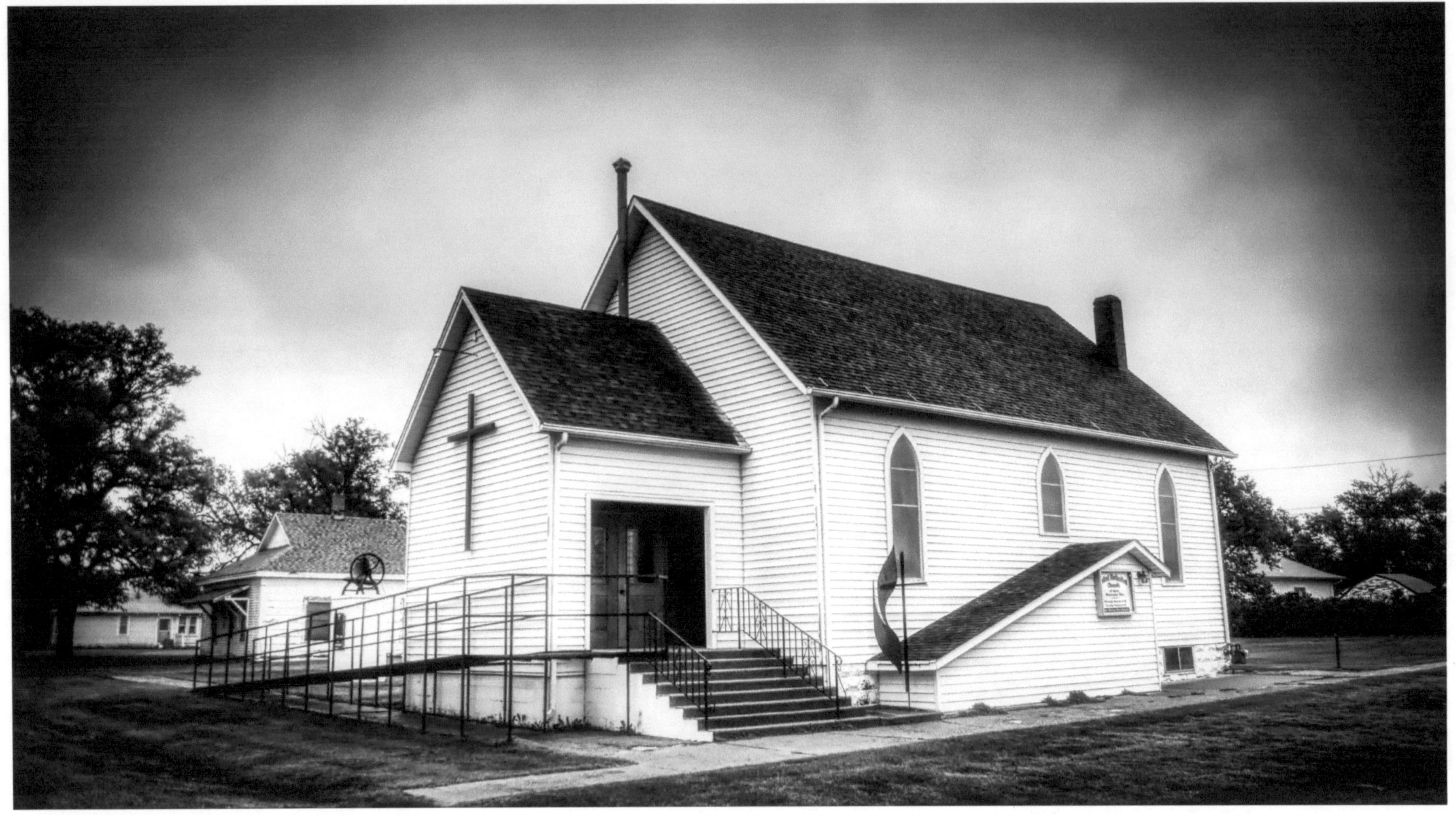

SACRED SPACE

PSALM 126 In convertendo

1 When the Lord restored the fortunes of Zion,
then were we like those who dream.
2 Then was our mouth filled with laughter,
and our tongue with shouts of joy

Here upon the high plains
Hidden in prairie dreams
Within an ocean of grassland
Inside sacred spaces where
Families and friends still
Gather across earth's seasons
To cherish the lives lived
A faithful confirmation
A reminiscence of rites
Where words left unsaid
Become the stillness of prayers
Often enclosed and mislaid
Murmuring anxiously in silence
As the world breathes one
More breath in a self-sufficient
Consecration now acknowledged
Intimate memories held in esteem
A sound of voices long vanished
Yet alive in holy communion
Giving birth to new litanies
How so often we come to rest

In a grace found inside
White wooden clapboards
Within these sacred walls
With a shy thanksgiving
In a community of confession
And endless reconciliations
O Lord — teach us please
How we might enter
Into the peace of all
Things upon the earth
And held holy in heaven
In words vivid with hope
Resting upon an altar
Bright with a promise still
Spoken to the world
To all humankind
So beloved and cherished
By Christ whom as teacher
Master and worshiped Lord
Frees us from the terrible
Hesitations of our hearts

UNITED STATES CENTER CHAPEL

Lebanon, Kansas

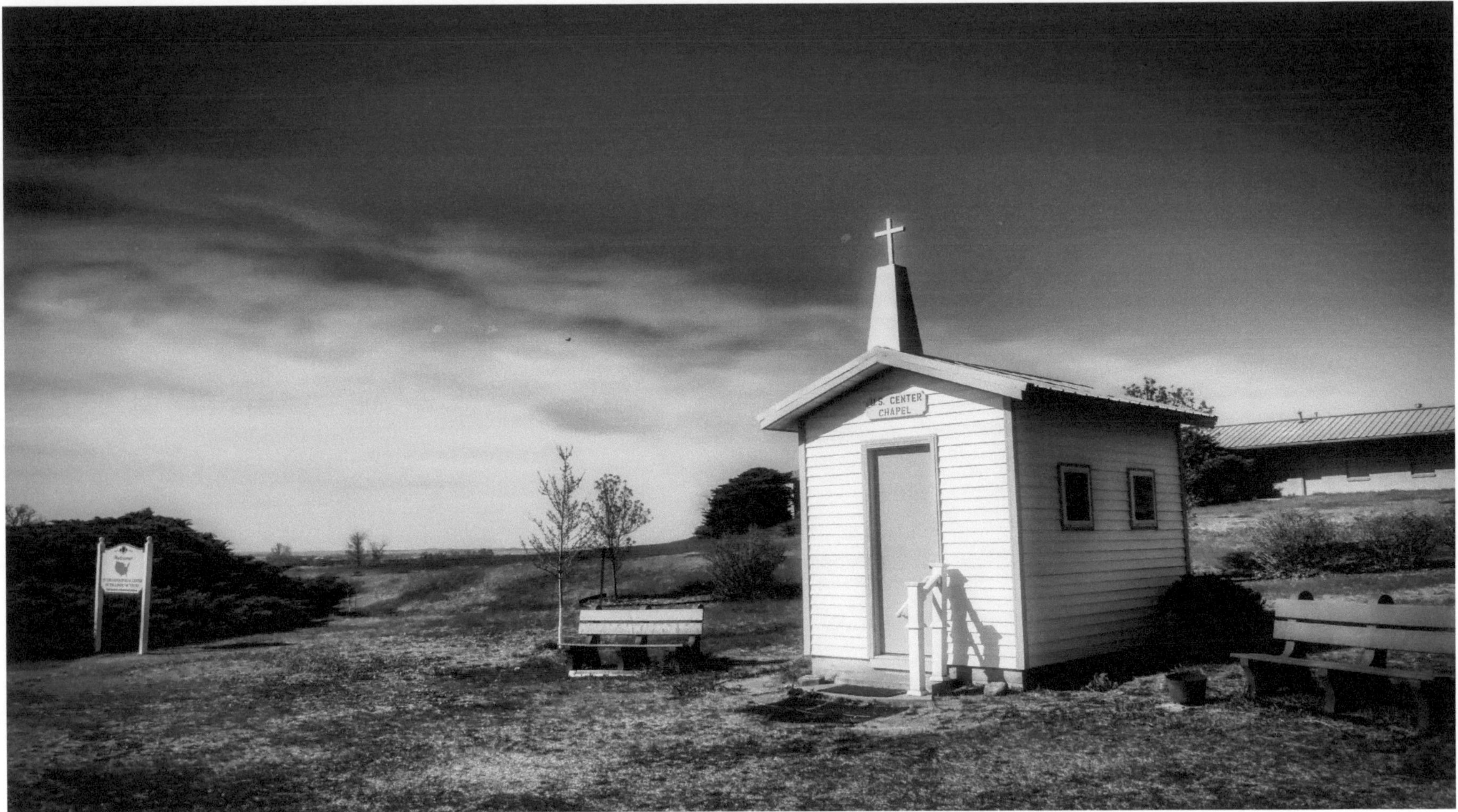

BEYOND MIDWINTER SPRING

MATTHEW 12 – (NRSV)

35 The good person brings good things out of a good treasure, and the evil person brings evil things out of an evil treasure. 36 I tell you, on the day of judgment you will have to give an account for every careless word you utter; 37 for by your words you will be justified, and by your words you will be condemned.

Beyond midwinter spring
When days are bright with sunlit hope
Where solitary dreams become a single
Dream of America — a promise fulfilled
Let us meet one another again
Without harsh words or brutal rhetoric
On this sacred ground in prayerful accord
O America attend our many voices
Let honored poets and storytellers speak
Across our history — spinning out
Verse after verse — story after story
Binding us together as a faithful people
Reconcile us from our tragic rage
And tyrannies of deceitful indifference
Let our cruelness wane — our enmities fade
Suspended in time between false and artificial
Discords washed away — given a new vision
As Christ restored sight to one born blind
Who made the deaf to hear and mute to speak
When he cried out "Ephphatha — be opened"
Stir our numb spirits in a Pentecostal flame
Burning away tired tongues and idioms
We bear this pain to know intimately
That in our suffering it is — we the people
In uncertain hours and broken foundations
Who must redeem history from human folly
And gain a unity within this blessed land
Where we are bound together as one
Out of many one — across prairies and plains
Over great mountains and hidden valleys
Flowing peacefully down streams and rivers
Running in resounding harmony
In landscapes and people freed
From our terrible hurtful hesitations
To become no longer immigrant
Or stranger toward one another
To discover ourselves once more
Returning to where we first arrived

UNITED STATES CENTER CHAPEL FARMLAND

Lebanon, Kansas

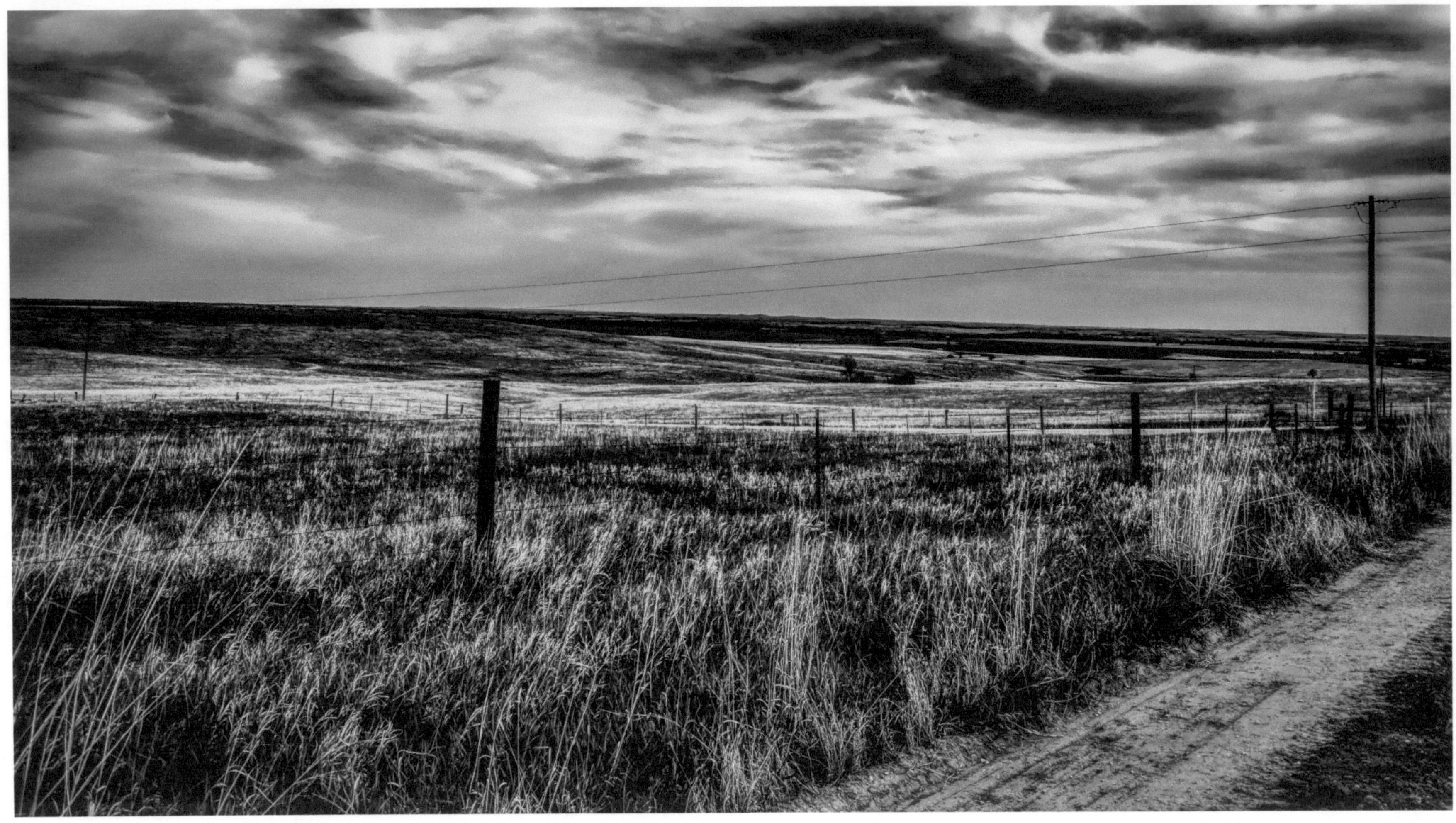

JOHN DEERE
Smith Center, Kansas

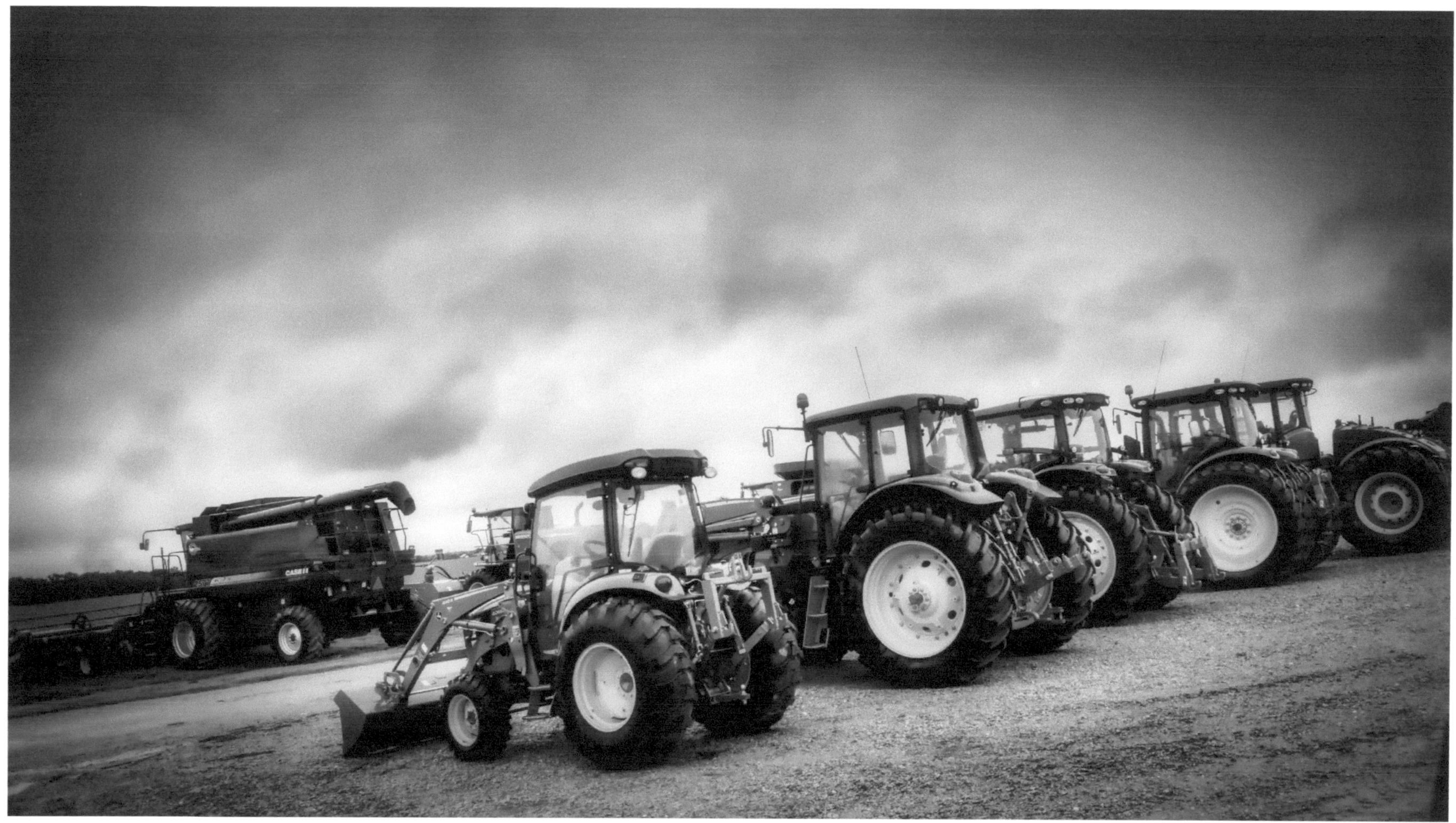

A Pilgrimage of Churches

The Great Plains

Glacial Hills of Kansas

PSALM 24 *Domini est terra*

1 The earth is the Lord's and all that is in it,
the world and all who dwell therein.

2 For it is he who founded it upon the seas
and made it firm upon the rivers of the deep.

3 "Who can ascend the hill of the Lord?
and who can stand in his holy place?"

4 "Those who have clean hands and a pure heart,
who have not pledged themselves to falsehood,
nor sworn by what is a fraud.

5 They shall receive a blessing from the Lord
and a just reward from the God of their salvation."

ST. JOHN LUTHERAN CHURCH
Easton Township, Kansas

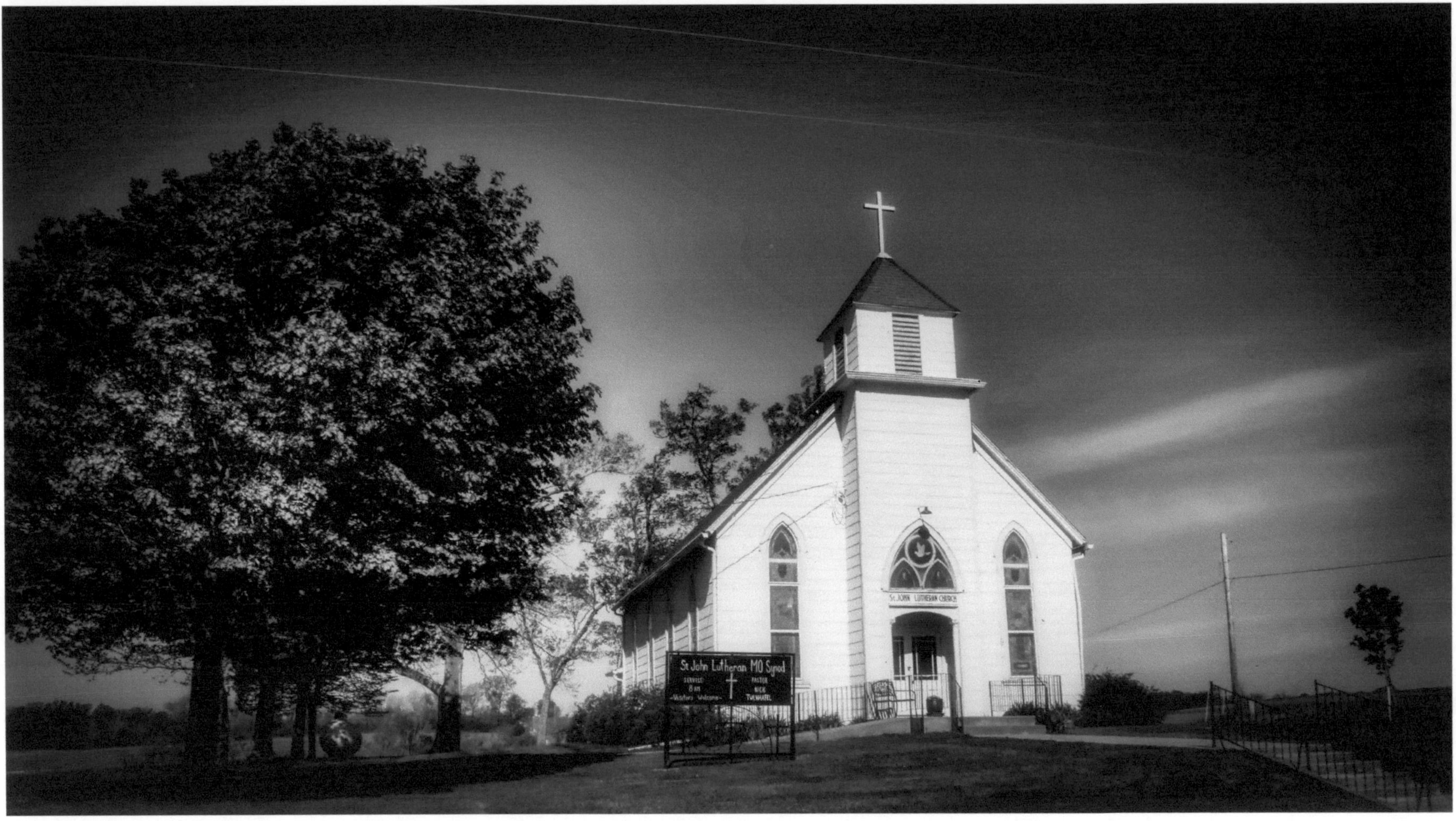

ST. JOHN LUTHERAN CHURCH

The Prayers of the People (Holy Eucharist Rite I – BCP)
Open, O Lord, the eyes of all people to behold thy gracious hand in all thy works, that, rejoicing in thy whole creation, they may honor thee with their substance, and be faithful stewards of thy bounty.

Before a new generation
Became a bright thought
Within creation's dominion
Blessing their ardent families
An impassioned gratefulness held
Fiercely in time's arched palms
Trusted without measure or means
Our kinfolk gathered together
As a body of faithful believers
To worship behind timber walls
Whitened with an intimate faith
An epiphany circling round
The promised years that vanish
Across pastoral landscapes loved
Adored beyond these viridian hills
Where a prairie wind brushes
Over the fluid sunlit wheat
Whispering within azure skies
To transform an evening light
Where celestial forms curve caringly
Over our many seasons and spells
Past troubled rain drought cyclone

How a voice calls forth to life
Treasured in the memory
Of all things revealed and hidden
In the seen and unseen spaces
Of heaven resting in creation
Accepting here its lenience
And respite from weariness
As a lovingkindness granted
An attendance unassuming
Vivid as the moon's complexion
An emergent compassion arising
A luminous wisdom long desired
And a novel consciousness
Balanced in serene holiness
A presence known across ages
In our remembrance given
Through grace hour by hour
Heard as a silent chant
An angelic chorus intoned
Without chance or recess
We may not know
We are even praying

ST. JOHN LUTHERAN CHURCH

Easton Township, Kansas

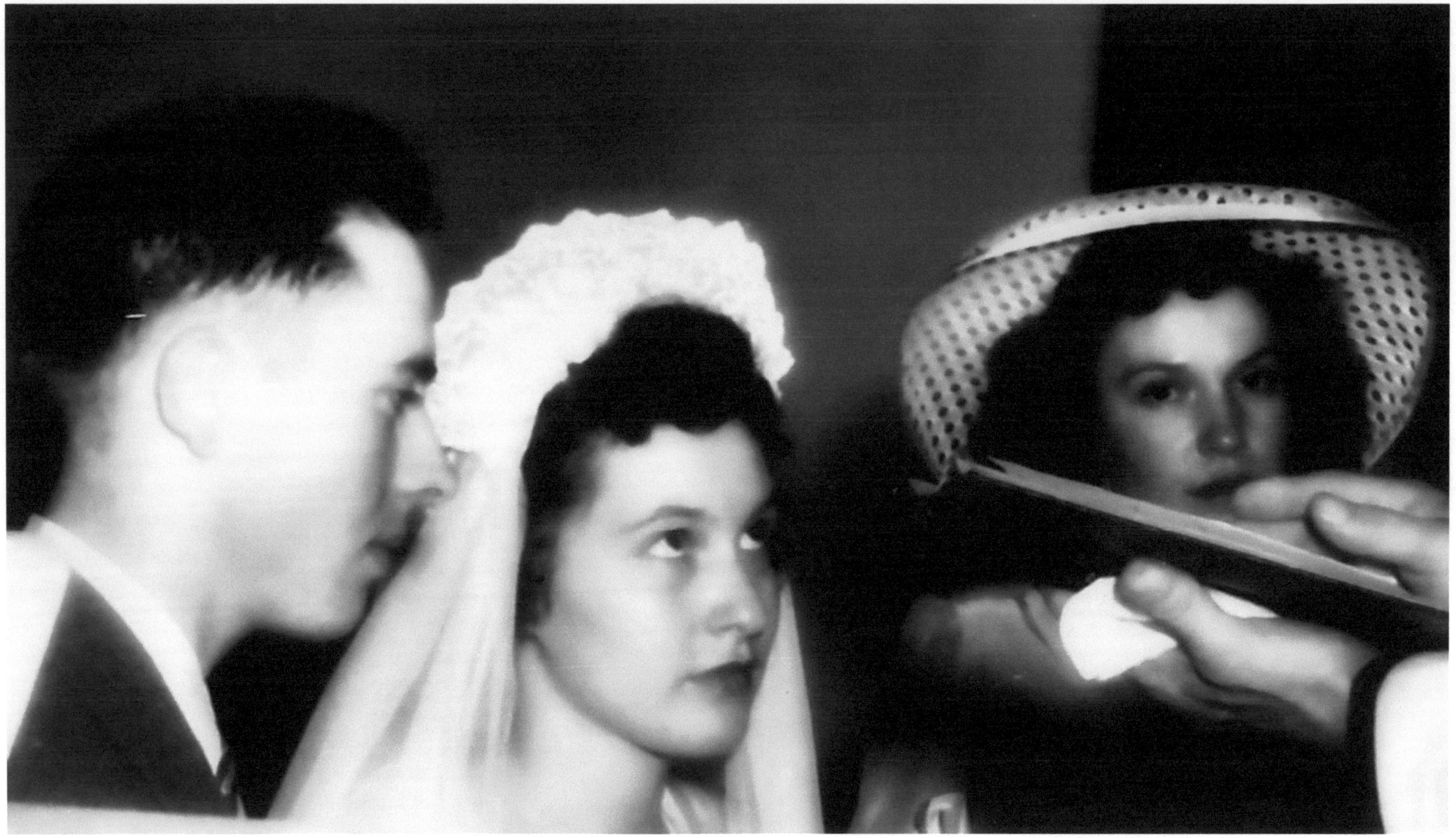

ST. JOHN LUTHERAN CHURCH

Easton Township, Kansas

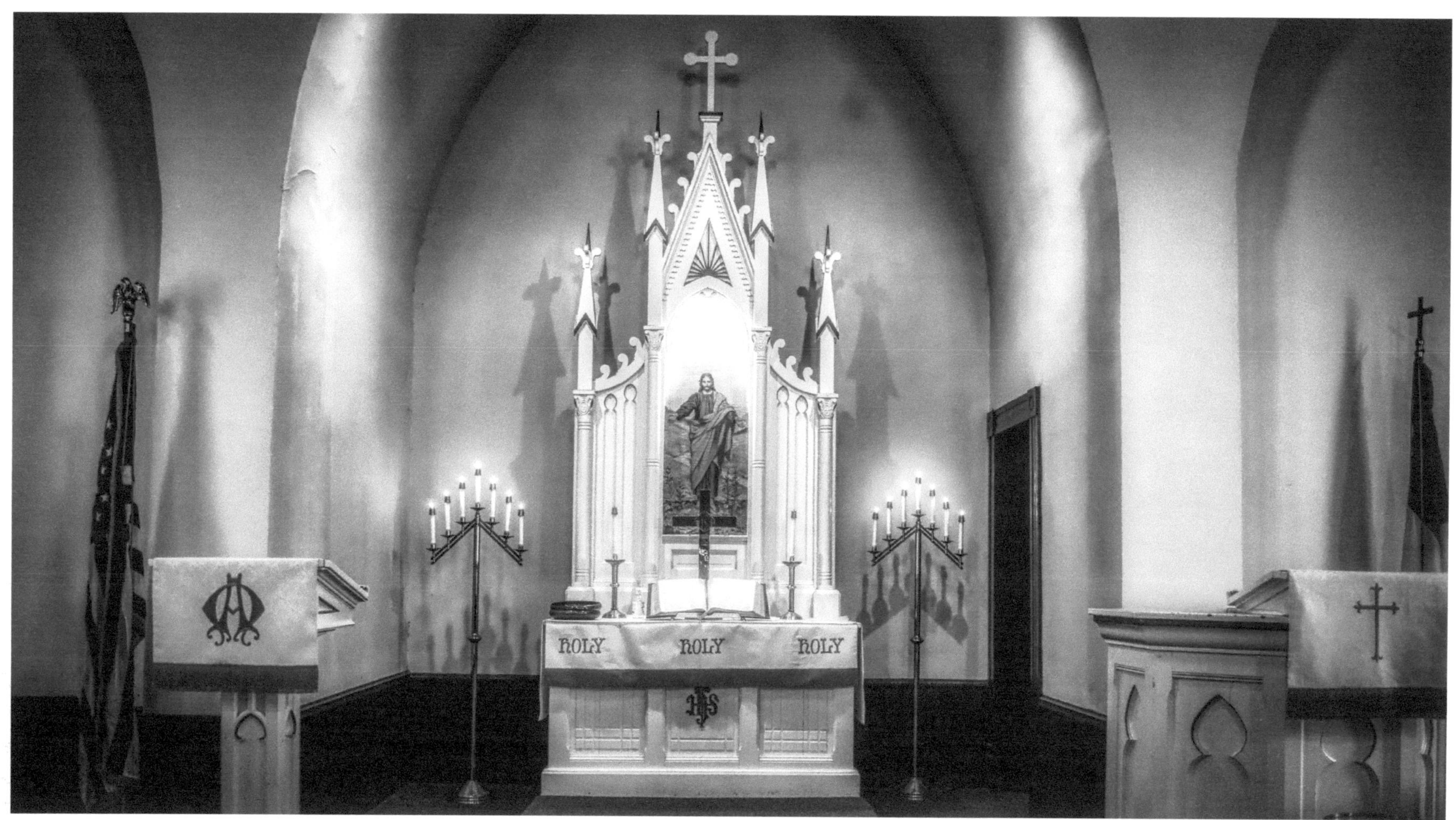

FAMILY HOMESTEAD
Easton Township, Kansas

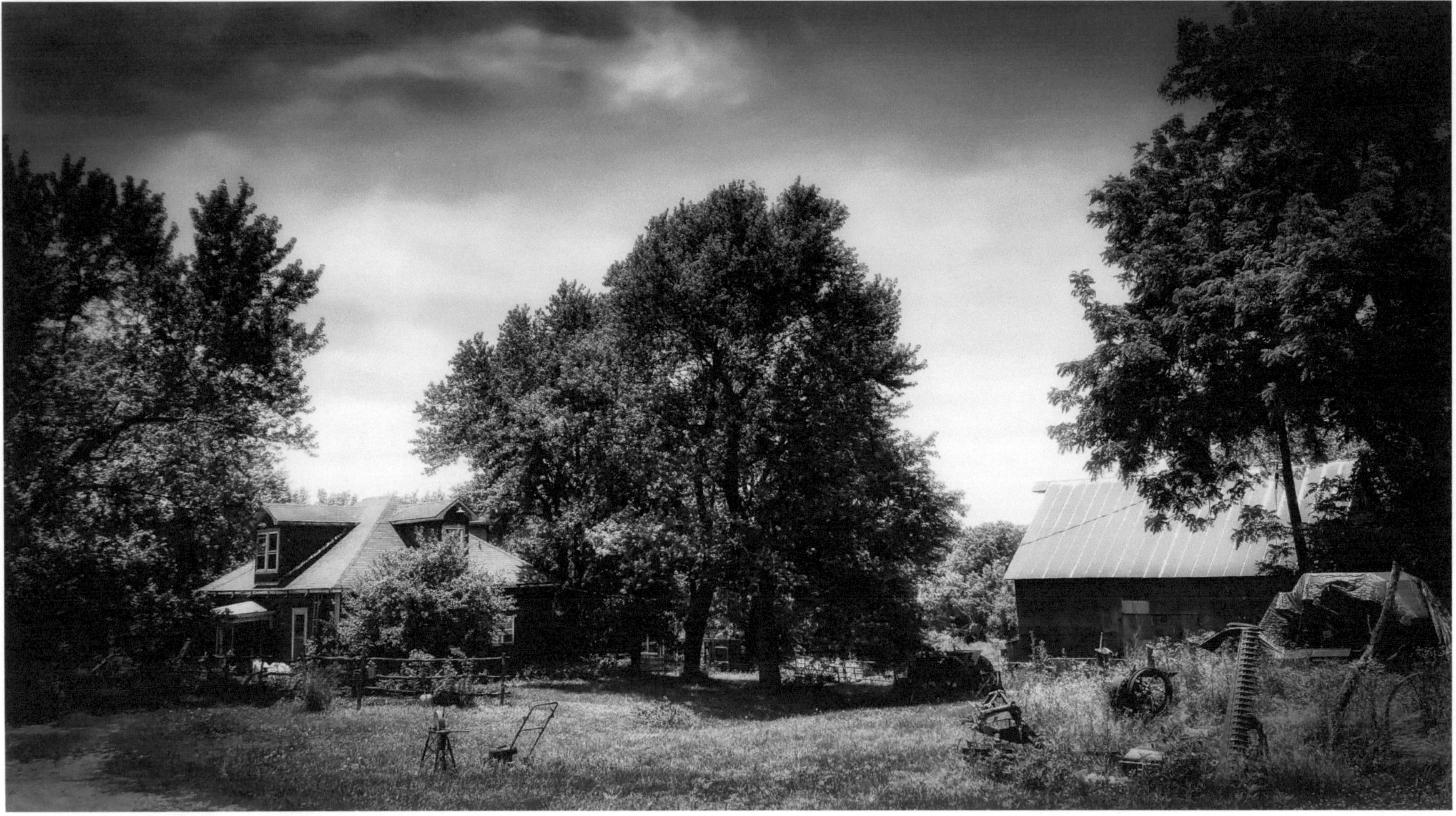

FAMILY HOMESTEAD

PSALM 91 Qui habitat

1 He who dwells in the shelter of the Most High,
abides under the shadow of the Almighty.
2 He shall say to the LORD,
"You are my refuge and my stronghold,
my God in whom I put my trust."

Today the prairie wind caresses
Curves upon an older face
Recalling a quiet wonder
The scent of apples and hay
Returns a wistfulness well-known
An eminent memory as *Mnemosyne*
Becomes our welcome guide
A gentle journey homeward
Childhood's innocent hours
Cherished since our infancy
Seasons ripened with a wild
Imagination rising limitless
So boundlessly assured of all
Things we revere on earth
And in heaven met and favored
Intuitively as we ran together
Beside smooth fluent rivers
Where Cottonwood and Elm
Reach toward heaven
Playing hide and seek
Through honey brushed fields
Of sun ripened winter wheat
Tasseled silken corn rows

Where harvest hopes flourish
On the surrounding Glacial Hills
Softened by a morning rain
Dancing across blue ponds
And flowing watercourses
Beside my grandparent's barn
Red–russet and flush with light
Where sorrel Missouri Mules
Once dwelled in dignity
Prized warmly by my grandfather
Traded now for draft horses
Leather tack and harness
Broad headed field collars
And sweet manure waiting
To be cleaned with care from
Wooden stalls worn smooth
Across the years with age
In this remembrance of what
Was and will be once again
We have grown wise in life
Drawn together in a youthful
Conspiracy of timely winds
Breathing the same kind air

ST. PAUL'S EPISCOPAL CHURCH

Leavenworth, Kansas

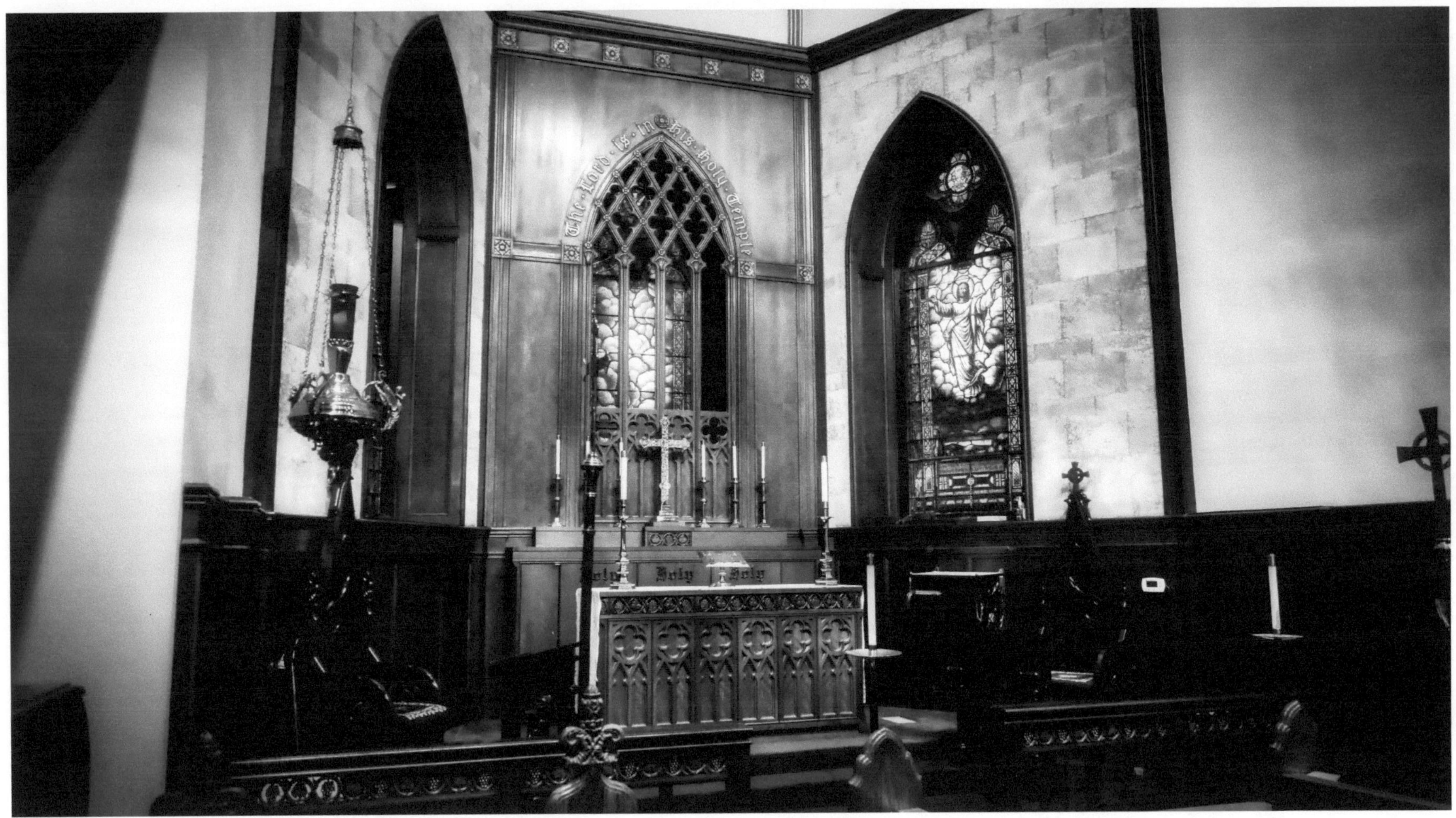

SANCTUARY LAMP

MATTHEW 5 – (AKJV)

16 Let your light so shine before men, that they may see your good works, and glorify your Father which is in heaven.

In the light from this lamp
We see the light of Christ
Shining into the world
For he is the Word first spoken
And the Word who speaks it
Whom takes the bread to break it
And takes the wine to bless it
As we who believe take it
The Word who becomes
The bread which is broken
And the Word who becomes
The wine poured out
And shed for us this day
In an everlasting moment
Upon all humankind
The Word made flesh
Both fully human and divine

Whom becomes our
Holy food and drink
In the consecrated
Bread and wine reserved
Under this light – including
All with weighty cause
Who cannot be with us now
Seeking a healing unity
In Christ's real presence
In this Eucharistic Feast
In this most Holy Mystery
Of new and unending life
Received by faith
And confirmed by love
Recalling his death
Resurrection and ascension
In an *epiclesis* light

BAKER UNIVERSITY CLARICE L. OSBORNE MEMORIAL CHAPEL

Baldwin, Kansas

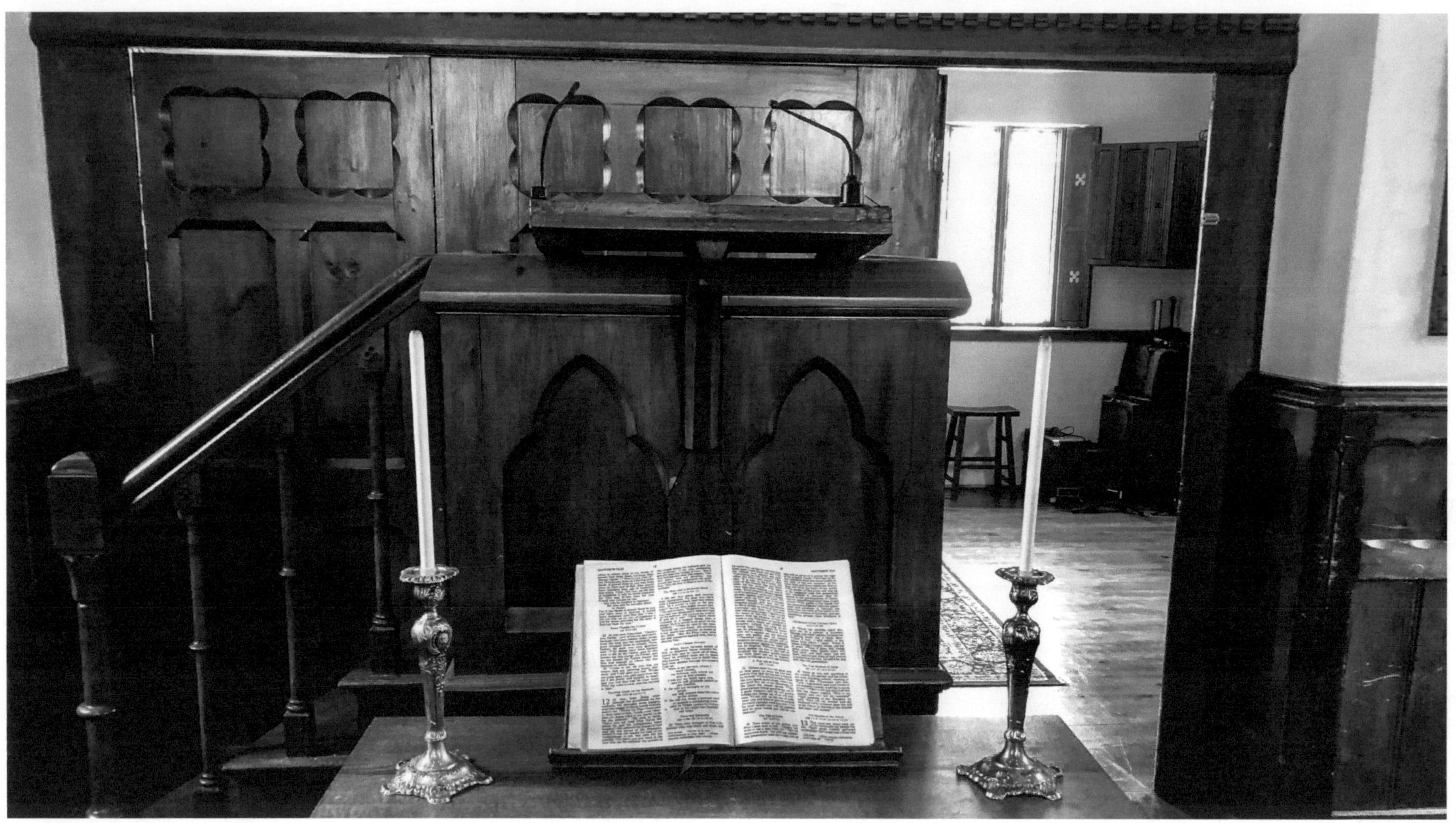

WISDOM BORN

WISDOM 6 – (NRSV)

12 Wisdom is radiant and unfading
and she is easily discerned by those who love her
and found by those who seek her.
13 She hastens to make herself known to those who desire her.

Voyage down these unfamiliar roads
Run with a radiance along clear
Flowing streams near sunlit waterfalls
Beneath calm shaded pathways
Teach humankind to follow wise
Beliefs and knowledges taught
O heroic journey where faith prolongs
Where dreams gather to fulfill history
Prophecies foretold which travel across
Our many years in fortune's space
Where time and vanity vanish
In an earthly humility ascending
From topsoil loam and humus
Across sacred landscapes
Singing out with a joyful noise
Where Tallgrass Prairies grow
Where assuring providence rests

Held motionless in silence
Witnessing where wisdom is born
In this treasured progress of faith
And learning shared as one
Listen to the owl who each dawn
Awakens knowledge and good counsel
Arousing songbird and angelic orders
To begin their ceaseless choral life
This wise and eminent commemoration
Along the passages we seek to travel
Down hidden corridors well met
Wisdom — may we soar together
Through the enormity of bare space
In an enduring and familiar flight
Traced across the heavens
Marking celestial movements
Unseen before by humankind

ST. MARY'S CHURCH

St. Benedict, Nemaha County, Kansas

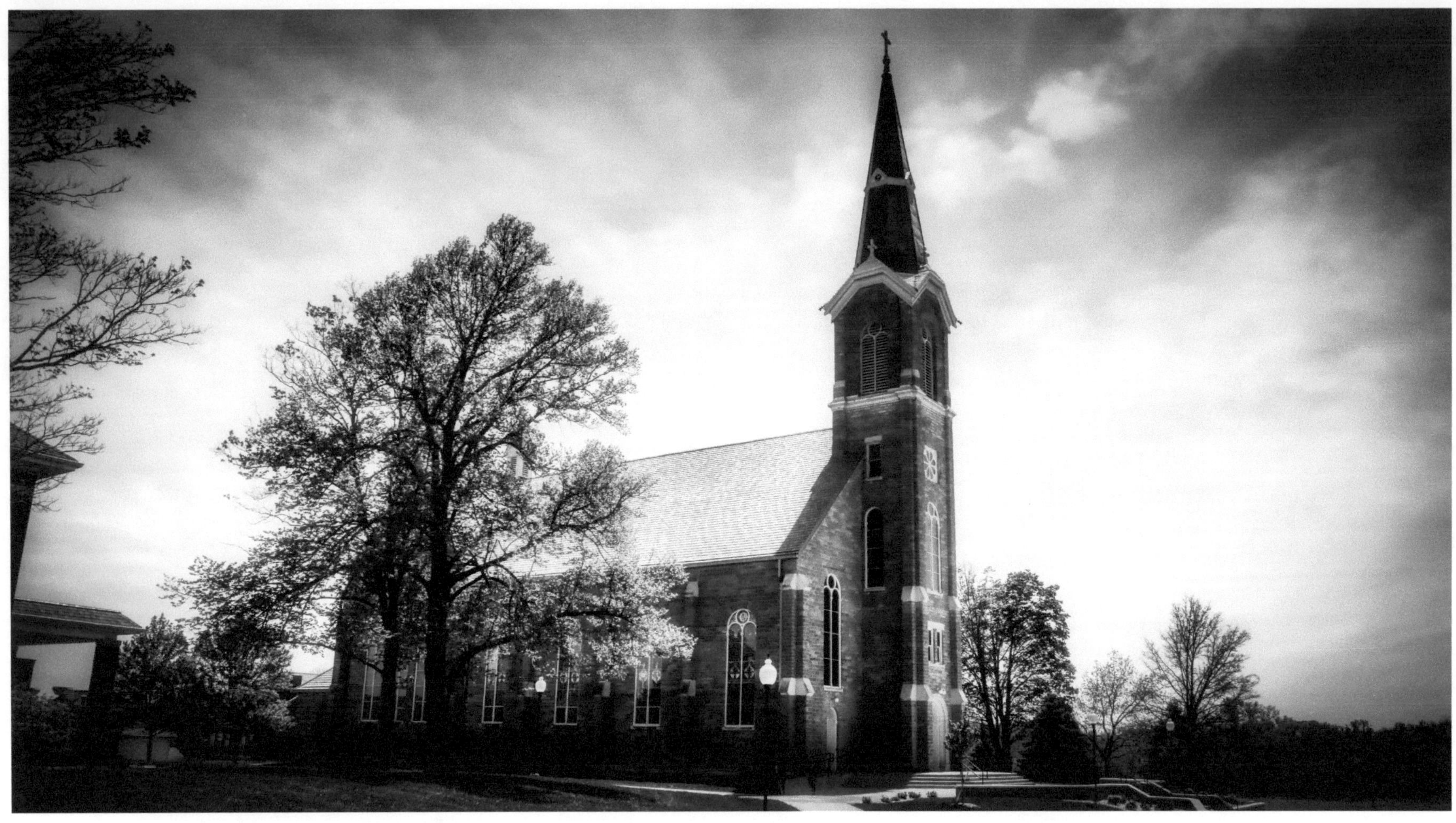

ST. MARY'S CHURCH

St. Benedict, Nemaha County, Kansas

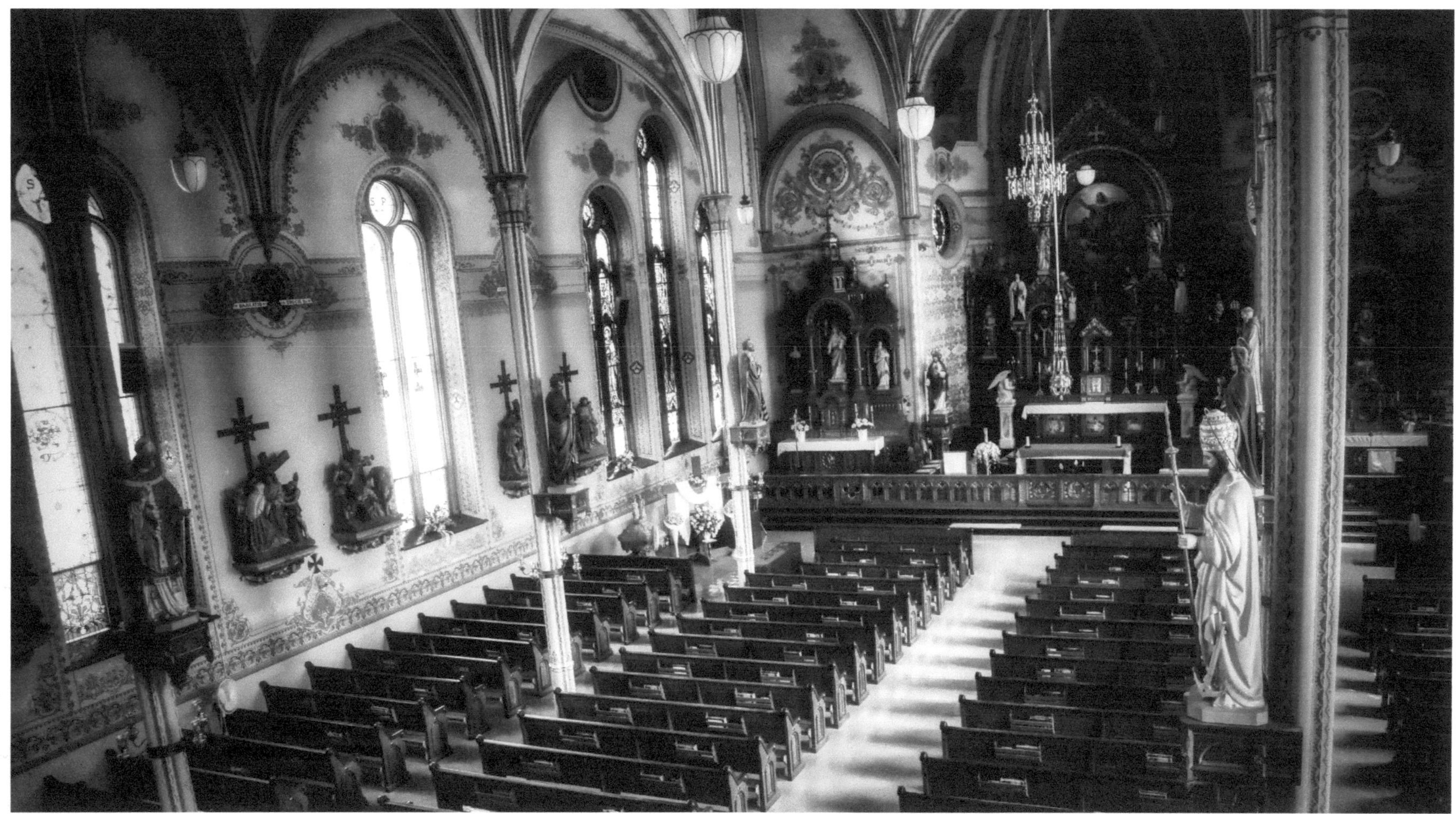

ST. THOMAS EPISCOPAL CHURCH

Holton, Kansas

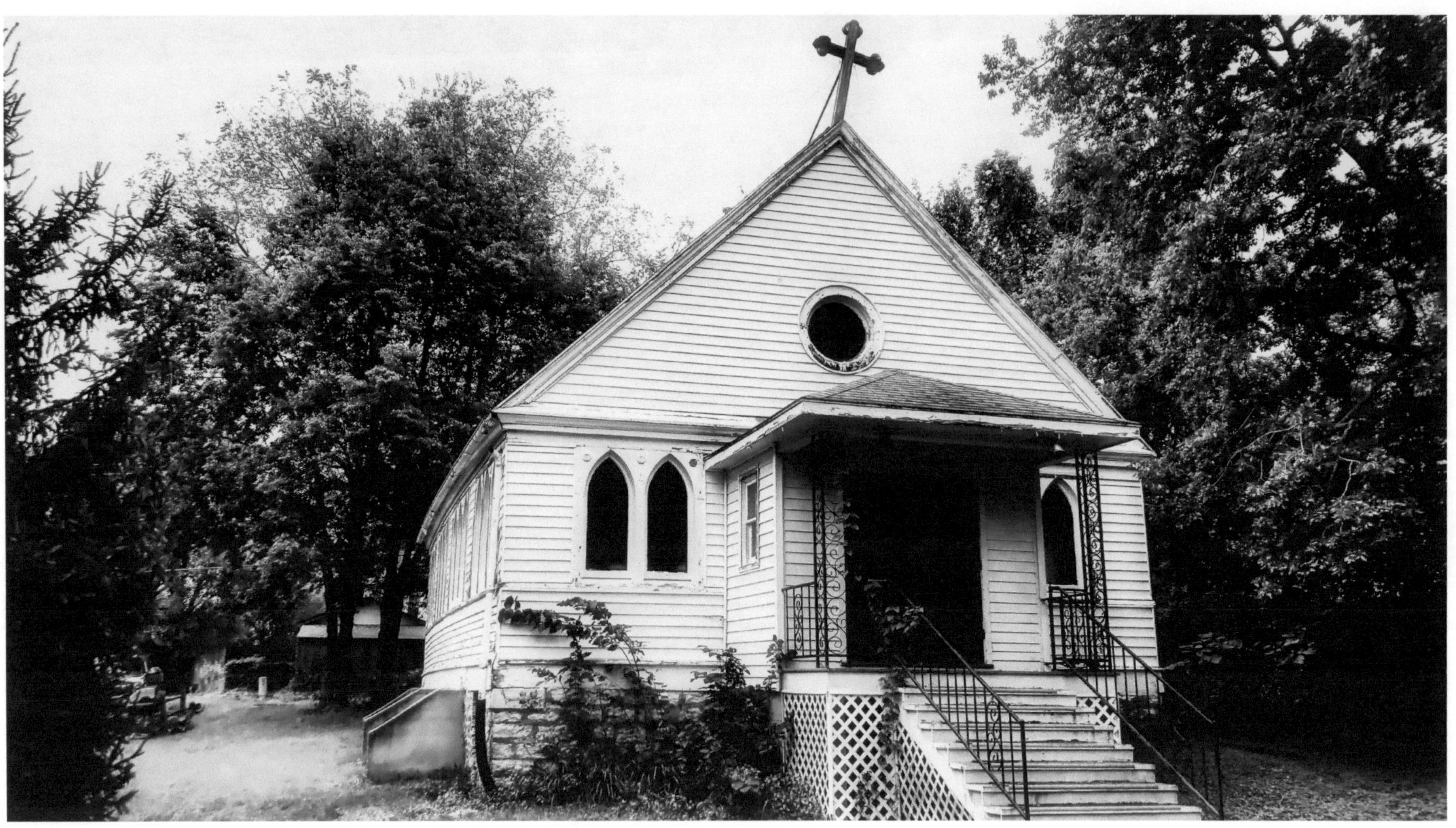

AN EASTER PEOPLE

ROMANS 12 – (NRSV) 2 Do not be conformed to this world, but be transformed by the renewing of your minds, so that you may discern what is the will of God–what is good and acceptable and perfect.

We are an Easter people
And *Alleluia* is our song
We are a people of God
Marked by the gentle coming
Of Christ in endless realms
Composed of many beginnings
And many endings in life
Embracing and engaging
With life – in its wonder
In its dying and rising
Up again once more
From the darkest places
Across time immemorial
Where all human thought
And memory becomes
Chronicled in heaven
As a remembrance where
Angels and archangels guard
The empty quantum spaces
Flowing through human hearts
Where prayerful thoughts
Perceive and create heavenly
Dominions without end
And allow vision – time to ripen
In faithfulness of mind

Pray without ceasing
Cast away all doubt
And release all deceptions
For we are what we imagine
Best an echo of our thoughts
Where the world arises
From belief and prayer
This is why scripture teaches
To let every thought be a prayer
Because from them we make
The world a better place
When we speak and act with
Love and compassion
Follow this sage advice
Take every thought captive
And your world will
Find a balanced bliss
So dwell on these things
Live in love and let it dispel
All animosity and enmity
This is the ancient law
Be swift to listen and love
Slow to speak with wrath
Be transformed day by day
With Christlike love

GOFF UNITED METHODIST CHURCH
Goff, Kansas

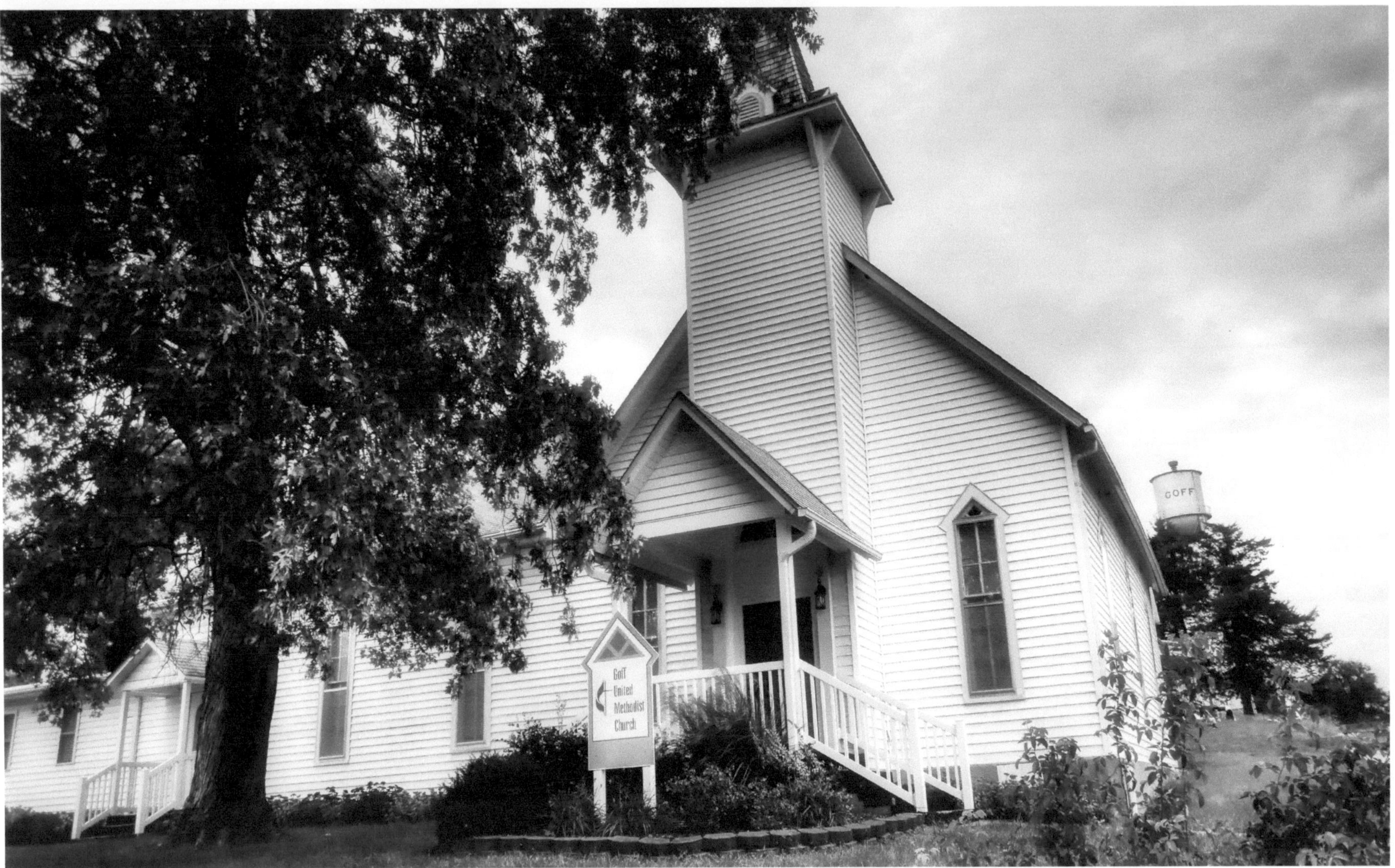

ALIVE WITH HOPE

PSALM 87 Fundamenta ejus

1 On the holy mountain stands the city he has founded;
the Lord loves the gates of Zion
more than all the dwellings of Jacob.
2 Glorious things are spoken of you,
O city of our God.

In Harrison Township
Nemaha County Kansas
People still live and rest
Among rolling treeless hills
Where Bluestem Prairie Grass
Once covered the whole landscape
Where water courses flow
Freely down Spring Creek
At a leisurely pace and time
Resting in timeless reveries
To nurture native plants
Where Scarlet-Orange Prairie Lily
Blue-Violet Blazing Star
Yellow Sawtooth Sunflowers
And Black-Eye Susan grow wild
Where Greater Prairie-Chickens
Build nests and raise broods
One generation after another
Tucked and hidden away among
Mixed-grass and Tallgrass Prairie
Standing regal upon modest hills

As homesteading families did once
And still do today in Kansas
On Sunday mornings they gather
Together as one community
To worship and sing praises
Forever known in their souls
Within these favored walls
Where stillness and silence
Rest and recognize a birth
Destined to transform the world
Shaking all the foundations
Of earthly means and desires
Arising humbly and faithfully
In this observance of a Holy Mystery
Generations before them knew
Intimately — cherished wholly
Without question with no need
To measure – holding no expectation
Alive with brilliant benedictions
To experience and be blessed
By God's brightened presence

WETMORE UNITED METHODIST CHURCH

Wetmore, Kansas

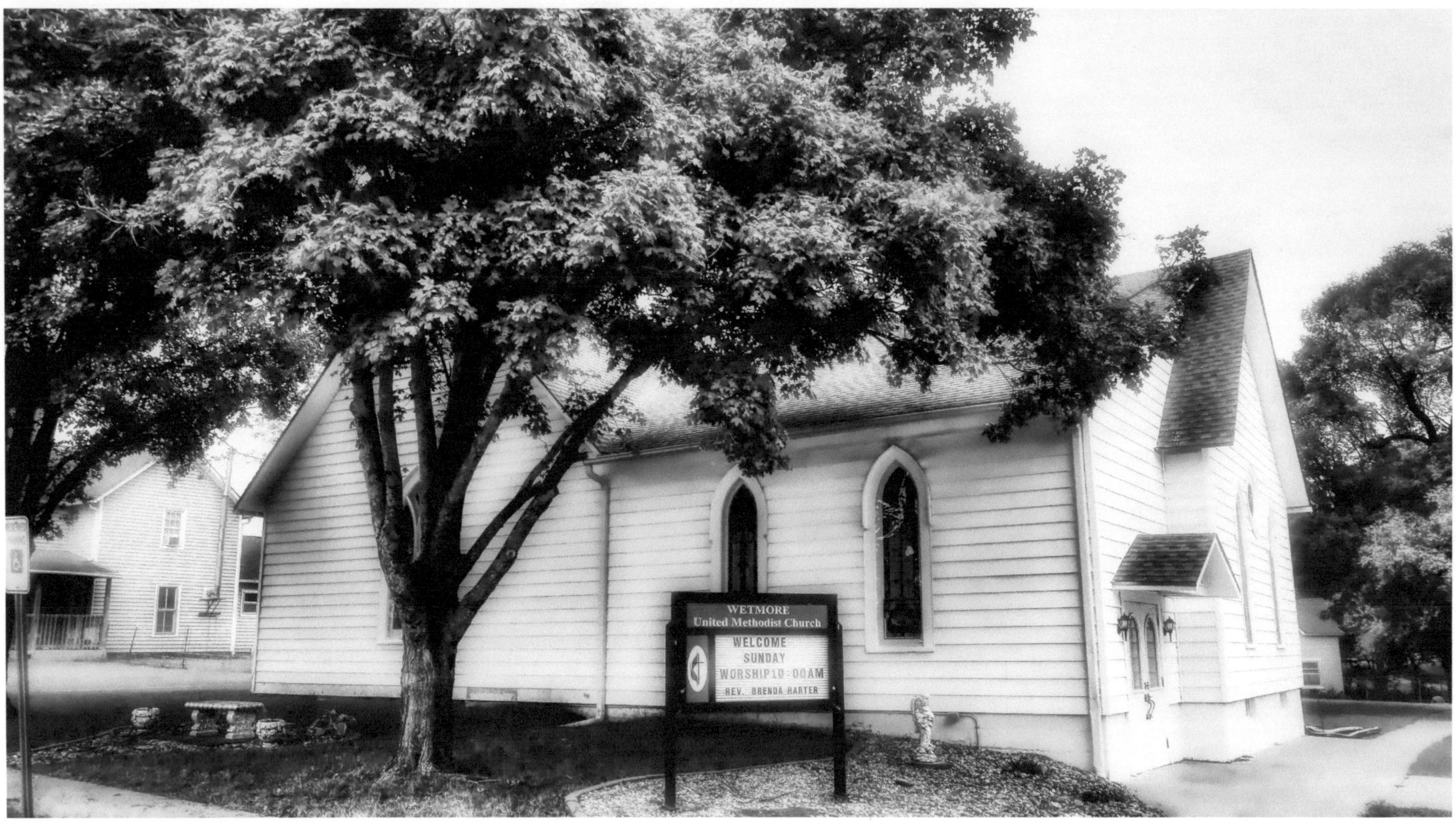

SILENT STARS

AMOS 5:8 – (BCP)

Seek him who made the Pleiades and Orion,
and turns deep darkness into the morning,
and darkens the day into night,
who calls for the waters of the sea,
and pours them out on the surface of the earth,
the Lord is his name,

Far above the light
Of heaven at night
Where angels and archangels
Sing together in one voice
United in prayerful unity
Where humankind discerns
The silent stars of creation
Floating on an indigo sea
Their iridescence pouring
Out across the Milky Way
Flowing from galaxies
Beyond our human ken
And humble knowledge
In a multiverse we barely grasp
Beneath this firmament
In greater mysteries invisible
To us now hidden inside
Our unceasing complexities
Of faith-filled learning and kind
Solitary luminous themes
Reflecting utterly and softly
Within one another's sight
Discovered inside the province
Of God's vision in midnight
Colors painted across the retina
As numinous streams traveling
Inward through vein and vessel
To spread incandescent upon
Blue-violet magenta washed
Waves swirling in time
And in space unseen before
Brilliant synaptic transmissions
Caressing nerve endings
We are naked in our trust
Floating in a greater memory
And remembrance of belief
Recalling something more of whom
We were before this moment
Surpassing the evening light
Vivid with God's presence
Bowing in prayerful affirmation
Arising now in gratitude and grief
Offered with sudden humility
Far from anxious passions
Marked by a gentler healing
And quickening of the flesh

WETMORE FILLING STATION MUSEUM

Wetmore, Kansas

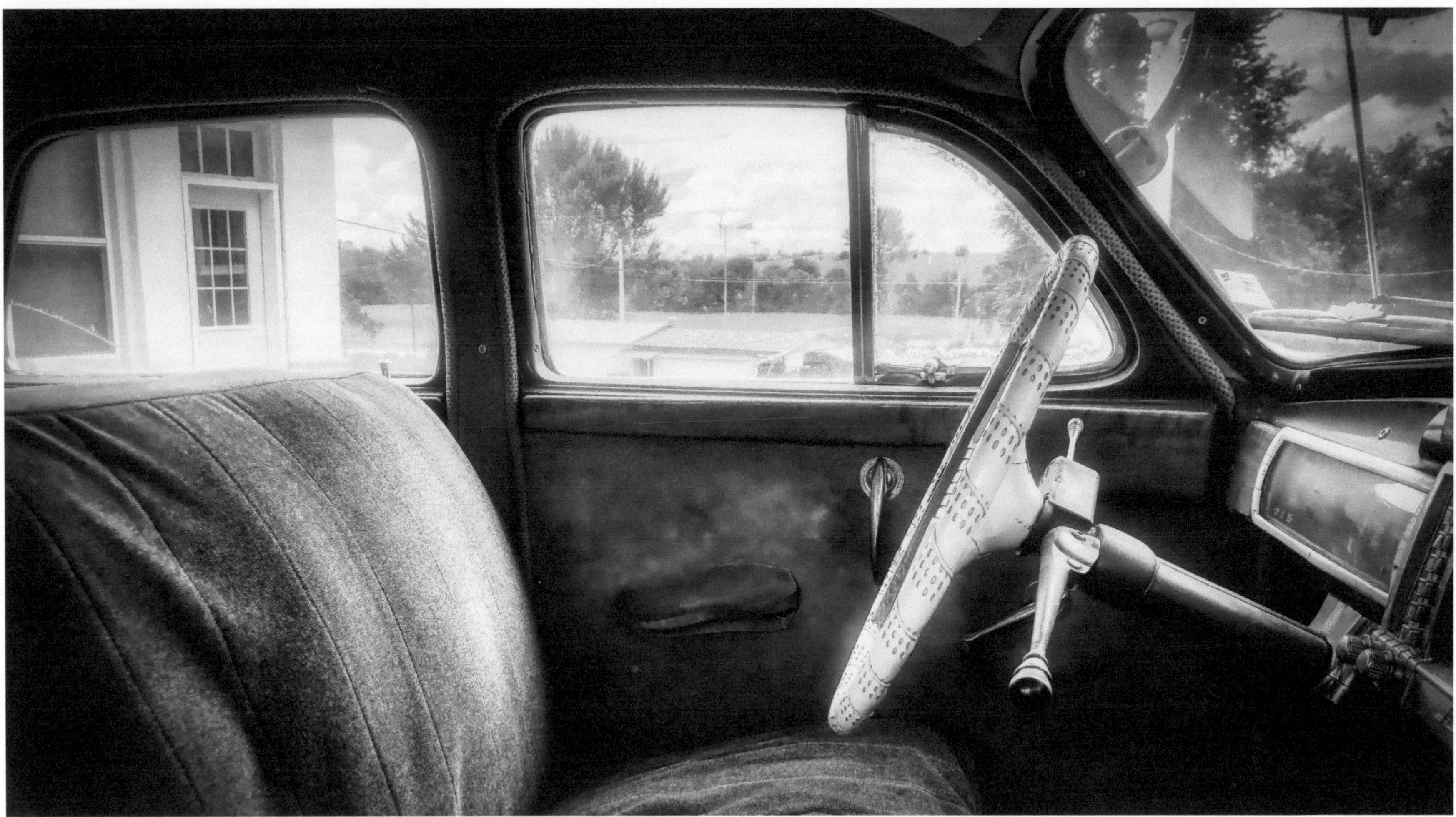

MARVELOUS REMEMBRANCE

PSALM 78 – Part I *Attendite, popule*
6 That the generations to come might know,
and the children yet unborn;
that they in their turn might tell it to their children.

I was born on the banks
Of the wild Missouri River
A dark bear — a massive brown
And muddy beast — pawing its way
In giant strides past deep woods
A totem animal and spirit guide
I still feel safe standing beside
Even today — the river is an old
Friend I try to visit often still
When I was only four or even
Five years old as time is told
My grandfather would come
To our home and gather me up
For a day of adventure and play
A time to see the wonder of the world
Fearless together — like Lewis & Clark
There was never a hesitation or fear
On my family's part to accompany him
We lived in a fair city long in history
And heritage alongside the high banks
Of the 'Big Muddy' where it bends
And turns southeasterly down
Towards the mighty Mississippi River

His old car a late 1940s model
Silver blue with whitewall tires
Where I rode shotgun
My grandfather driving beside
Me — smelled of cool aftershave
Lotion and fresh cigar smoke
The hood and fenders shimmered
And polished with light
From freshly applied car wax
Brightly buffed to shine and glow
As we glowed inside whenever
We kept company together
This is the wonderous thing
About all grandparents
And aunts and uncles too
We spoil children in their earliest
Years — showing them in flashes
The marvelous wonders
Of a world without end
Creating a wonder inside them
Lasting a lifetime and beyond
To share with the next
Generation to be born

WETMORE FILLING STATION MUSEUM

Wetmore, Kansas

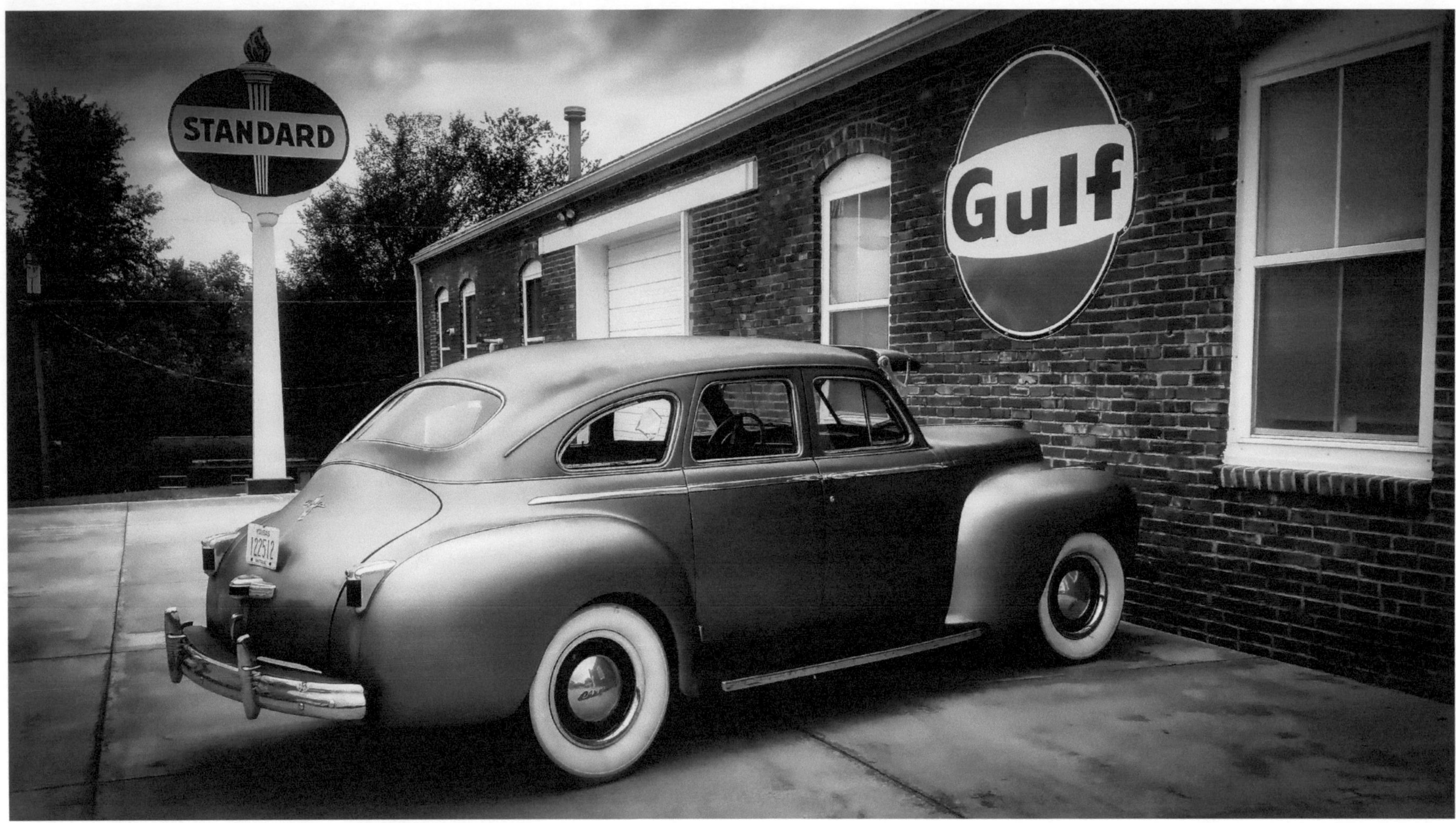

WETMORE FILLING STATION MUSEUM

Wetmore, Kansas

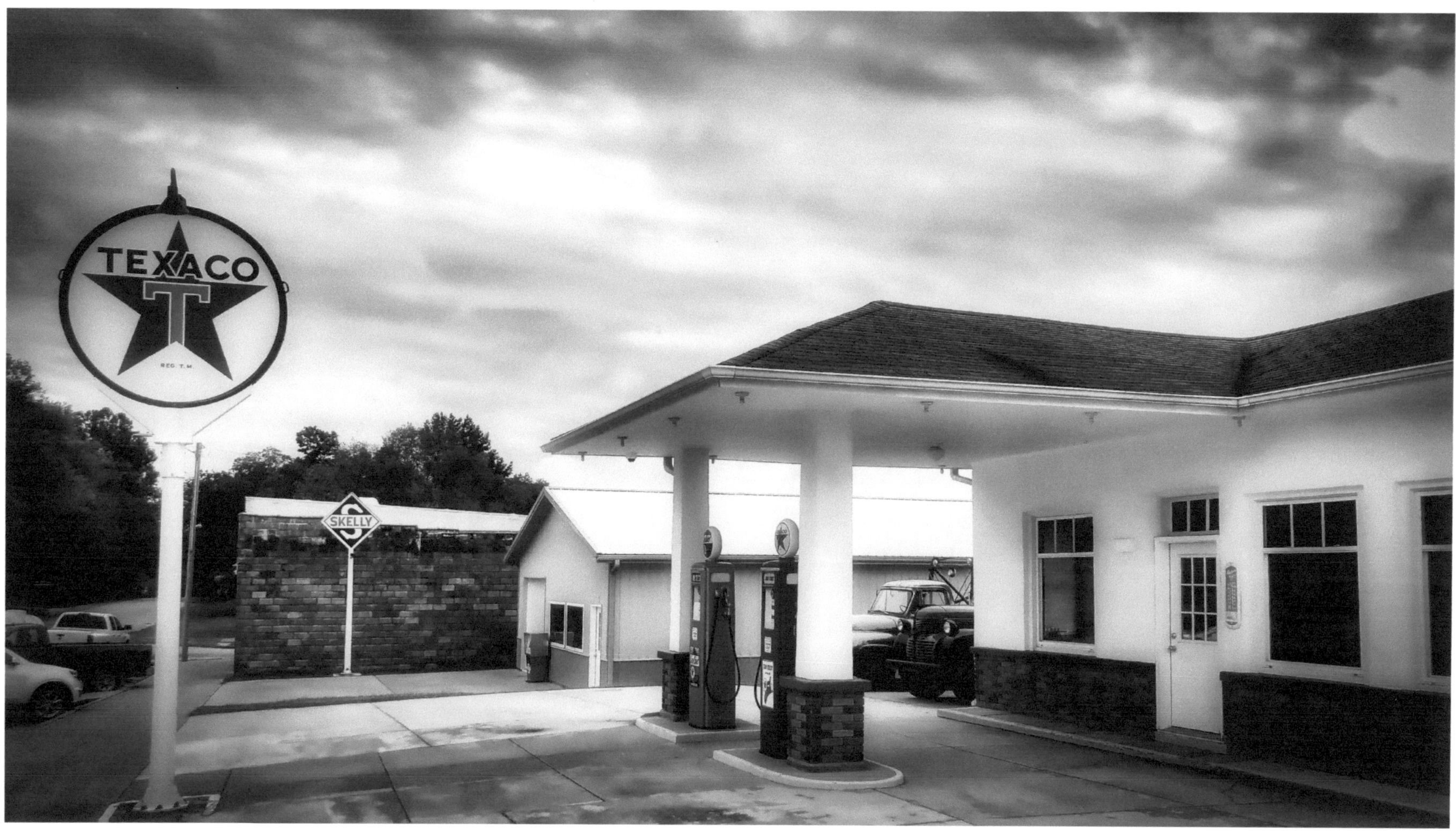

A Pilgrimage of Churches

The Great Plains

Flint Hills of Kansas

PSALM 33 *Exultate, justi*

12 Happy is the nation whose God is the Lord!
happy the people he has chosen to be his own!

13 The Lord looks down from heaven,
and beholds all the people in the world.

14 From where he sits enthroned he turns his gaze
on all who dwell on the earth.

15 He fashions all the hearts of them
and understands all their works.

OLSBURG UNITED METHODIST CHURCH
Olsburg, Kansas

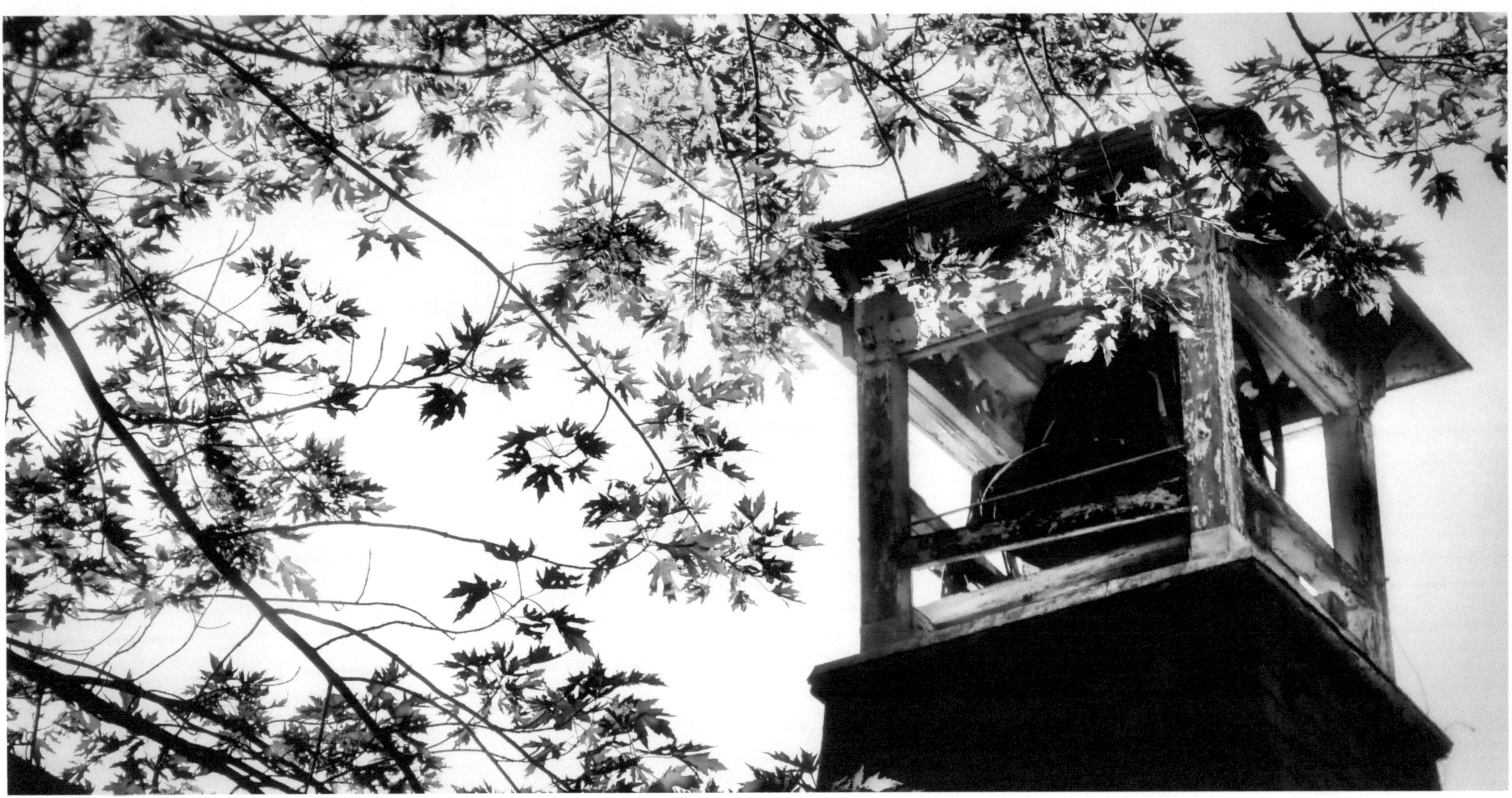

OLSBURG BELL TOWER

PSALM 118   *Confitemini Domino*
28 "You are my God, and I will thank you;
you are my God, and I will exalt you."
29 Give thanks to the LORD, for he is good;
his mercy endures for ever.

In our memory is a song
Ringing from an old bell tower
Raised high a hundred years ago
By another faithful generation
Honoring those who conceived
A church laid with shingles
And a sapling once planted
Grown taller now brushes softly
Against aged wood to cast shadows
Where peeling paint and light
Reflecting from russet autumn
Leaves catch and enter our eyes
So that our mind turns gently
Towards the light where waiting
In thoughtful simplicity of heart
The pure stillness and silence
Of our modest mortal flesh
Signals an imminent prophet

Envisioning our healing
Beyond the ruined places
Of our human hearts
Where voices raised in reverence
Welcome this holy mystery
Cherished long since childhood
Dwelling here in plenty
O Lord open our eyes
To trace your vital presence
An ancient *anáphora* spoken
In this eucharistic feast
As a sacramental *epiclesis*
Present in this bread and wine
Residing everywhere within
Our fragile broken world
An everlasting grace we recall
Where your holiness rings true
In this tribute of faith

OLSBURG UNITED METHODIST CHURCH
Olsburg, Kansas

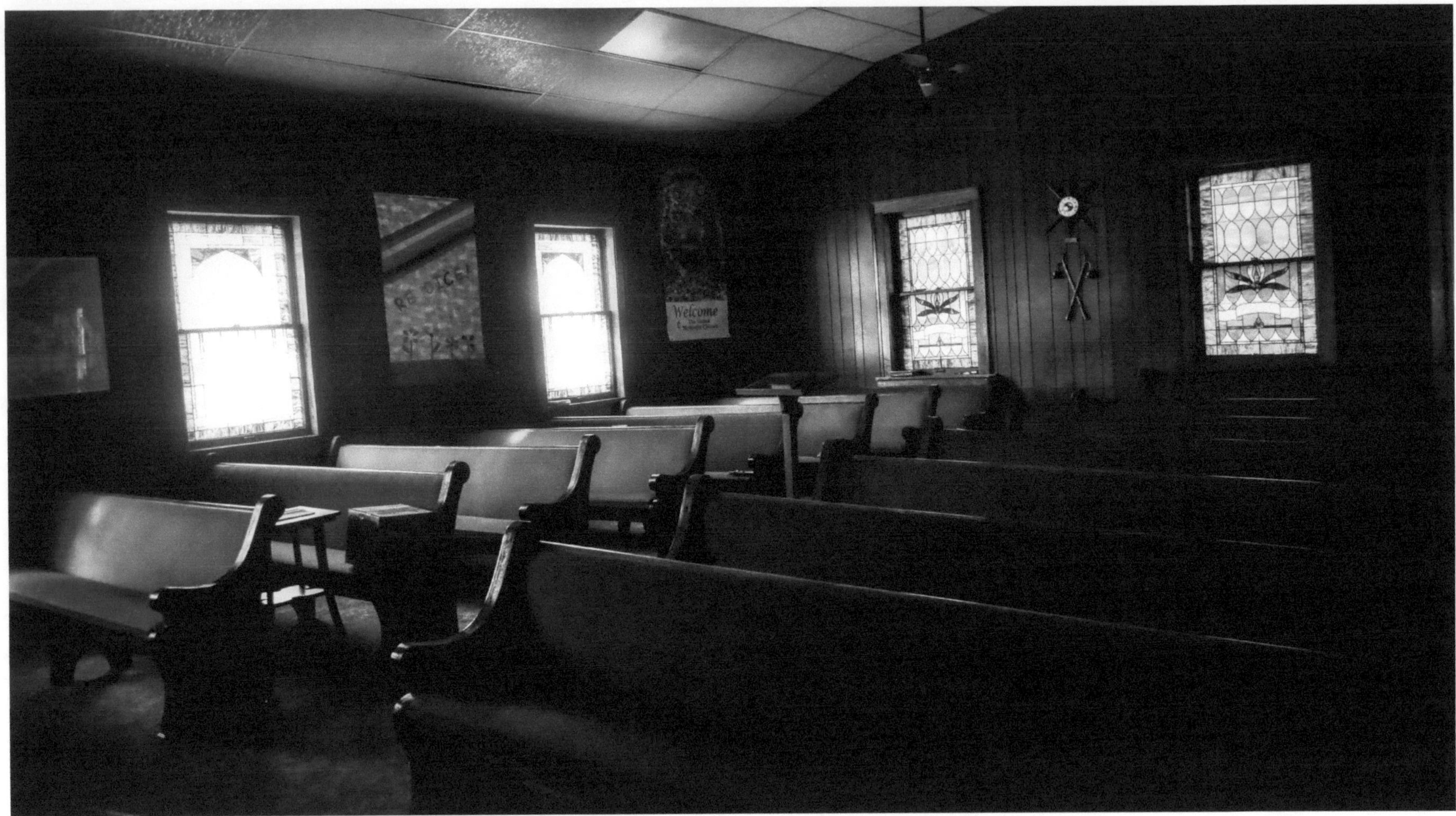

WESTMORELAND UNITED METHODIST CHURCH

Westmoreland, Kansas

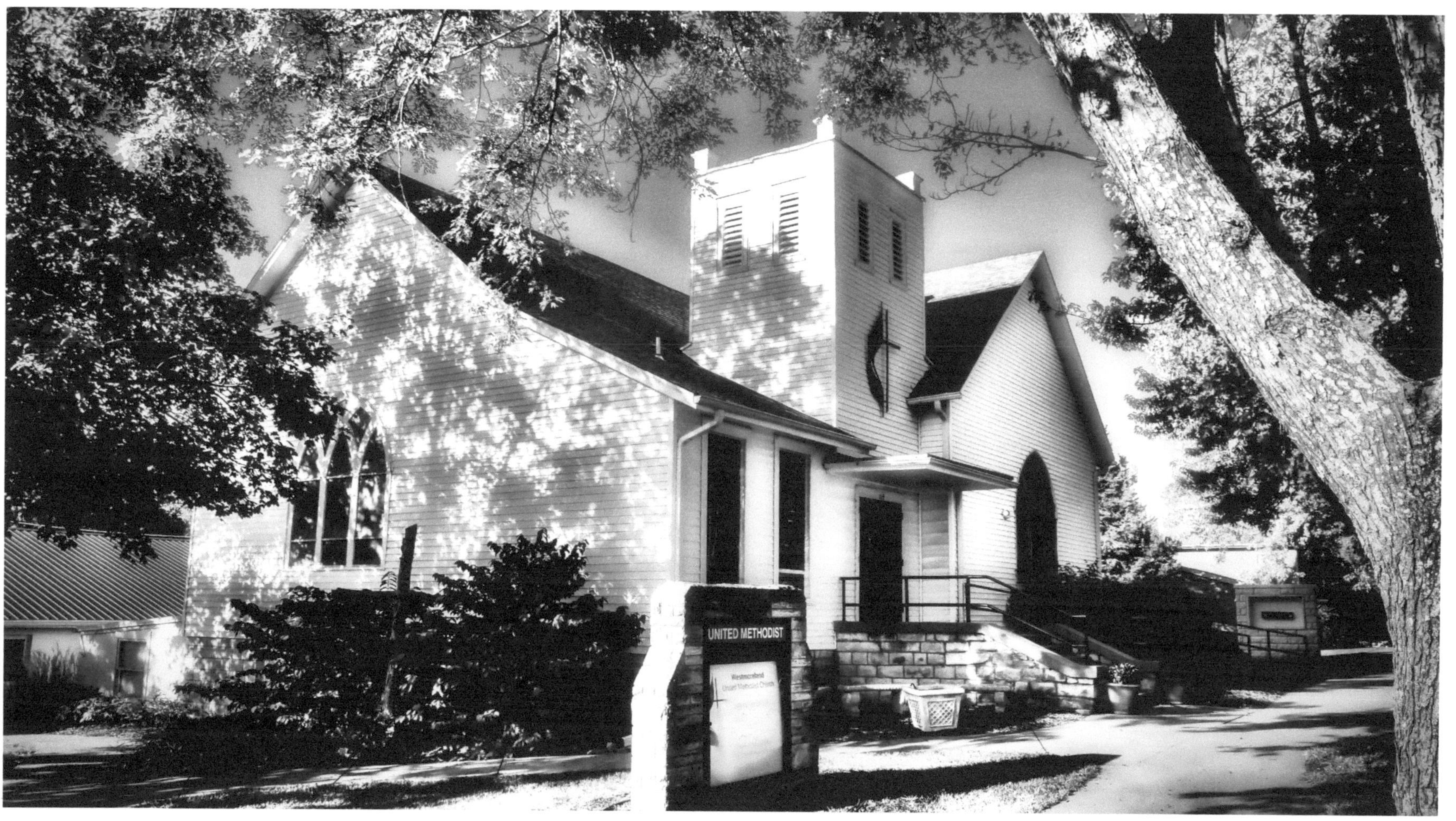

WESTMORELAND UNITED METHODIST CHURCH
Westmoreland, Kansas

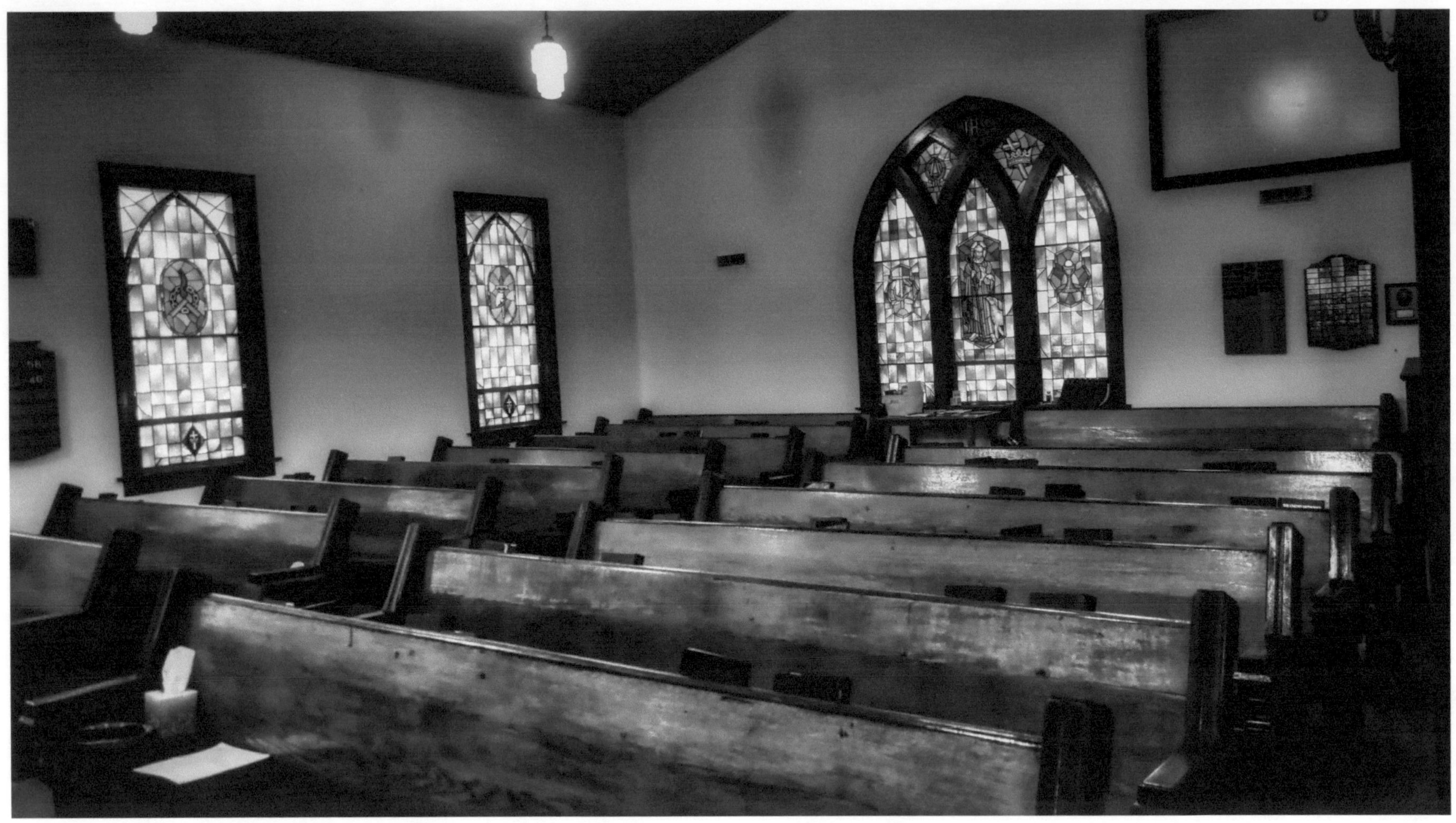

LIVING THE GOSPEL

MATTHEW 11 – (AKJV)

30 For my yoke is easy, and my burden is light.

The story in this church
Is this — the people are waiting
For the Second Coming
But no one really knows
When that will be . . .
It could be at any
Hour of any day
Today or tomorrow
Or a thousand
Or two thousand years
From now or even more
Meanwhile — God is smiling
And sends plenty
Of work their way
He is simply asking
Them to love one another
To feed his sheep
Day in and day out

So — this is what they do
This is the body of Christ
At work within the world
Within their world
They love the world
As best they can
With what they have
To honor this New Creation
And the New Being
Found in Christ their Lord
Here they have found
Rest for their souls
They have found that
Their yoke is easy
And their burdens light
They have found
That they are singing
Alleluias without end

OKETO UNITED METHODIST CHURCH

Oketo, Kansas

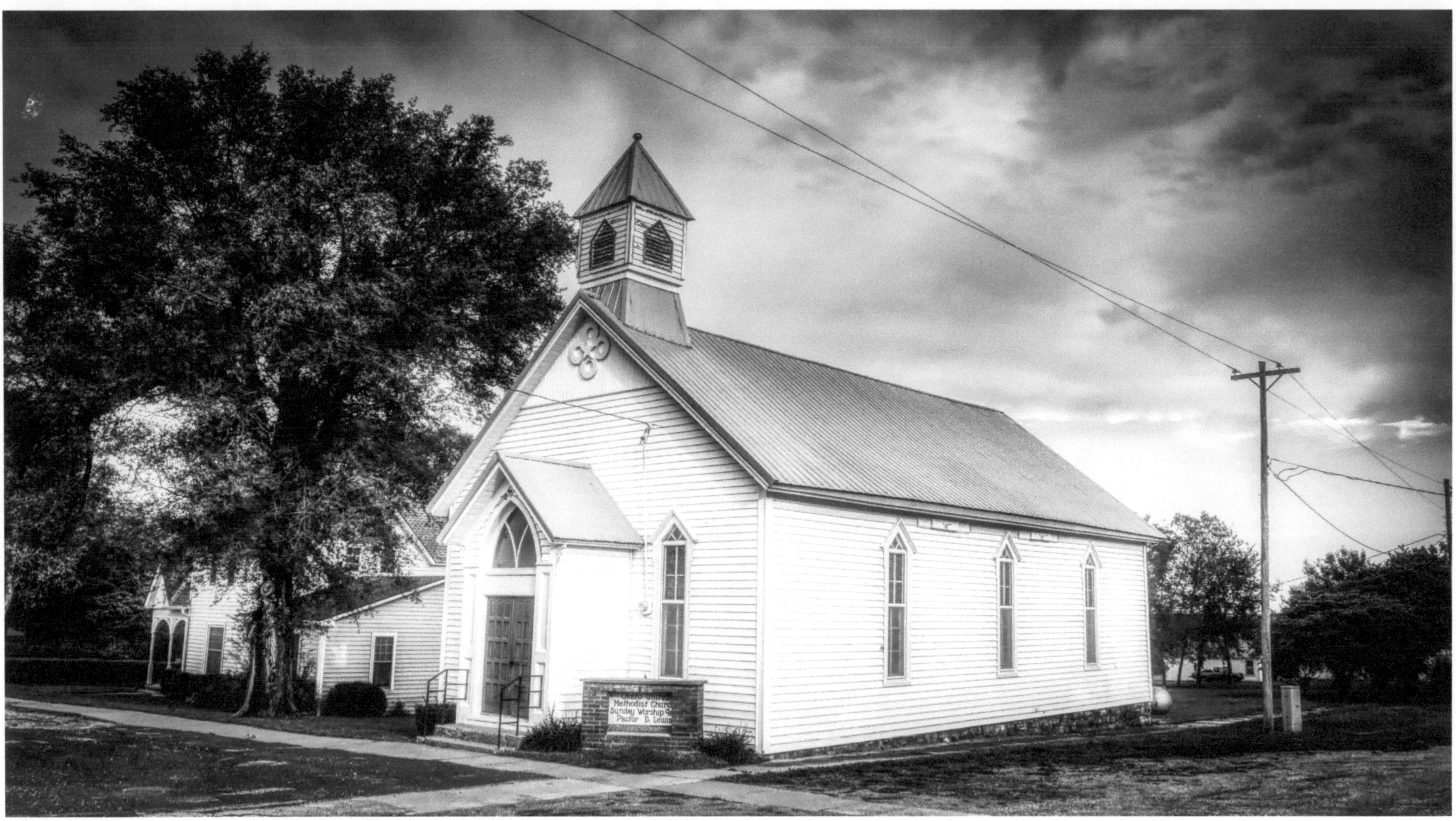

THANKSGIVING EVE

WE GATHER TOGETHER (1894 Translation by Theodore Baker)
We gather together to ask the Lord's blessing;
he chastens and hastens his will to make known;
the wicked oppressing now cease from distressing:
sing praises to his name; he forgets not his own.

When I consider joyful gatherings
In a harvest season blessed
With maize and winter squash
Apple cider cold from frost
And the seasonal pome press
Beneath scarlet tinged maples
Burning in crimson fires
And amber lights wedded
To one another beyond ken
Seared in saffron flames
Shimmering with anticipation
On a Thanksgiving Eve amid
Faith filled memories we recall
And bring forth once more
To renew the Spirit's warmth
Within our mortal frailness
Bearing a gentle gratitude
And the foreseen advent
Given now on sabbath dawn
Awaiting in expectation
Even as our human sorrow
Is sown beside our gladness
To become a kindness grown
A luminous joyfulness known

A grief turned by *Aion's* myth
To an enduring courage
An autumn space we reap
After such anxious plantings
Left in the earth to flourish
Healed by timely patience
Released by forces unforeseen
Capturing our human longing
Only eternity's promise may
Fulfill amidst all its wonder
Such infinite possibilities
So then we must discern
When time fades from illusion
And yet – let us not forsake
This earthly light too soon
Let it be known with some
Degree of certainty granted
Grounded in the body
Human beings cannot always
Endure what we see as eternal
Only through death and living
May we come to know
Creation as intransient
Consciousness as stillness

OKETO UNITED METHODIST CHURCH
Oketo, Kansas

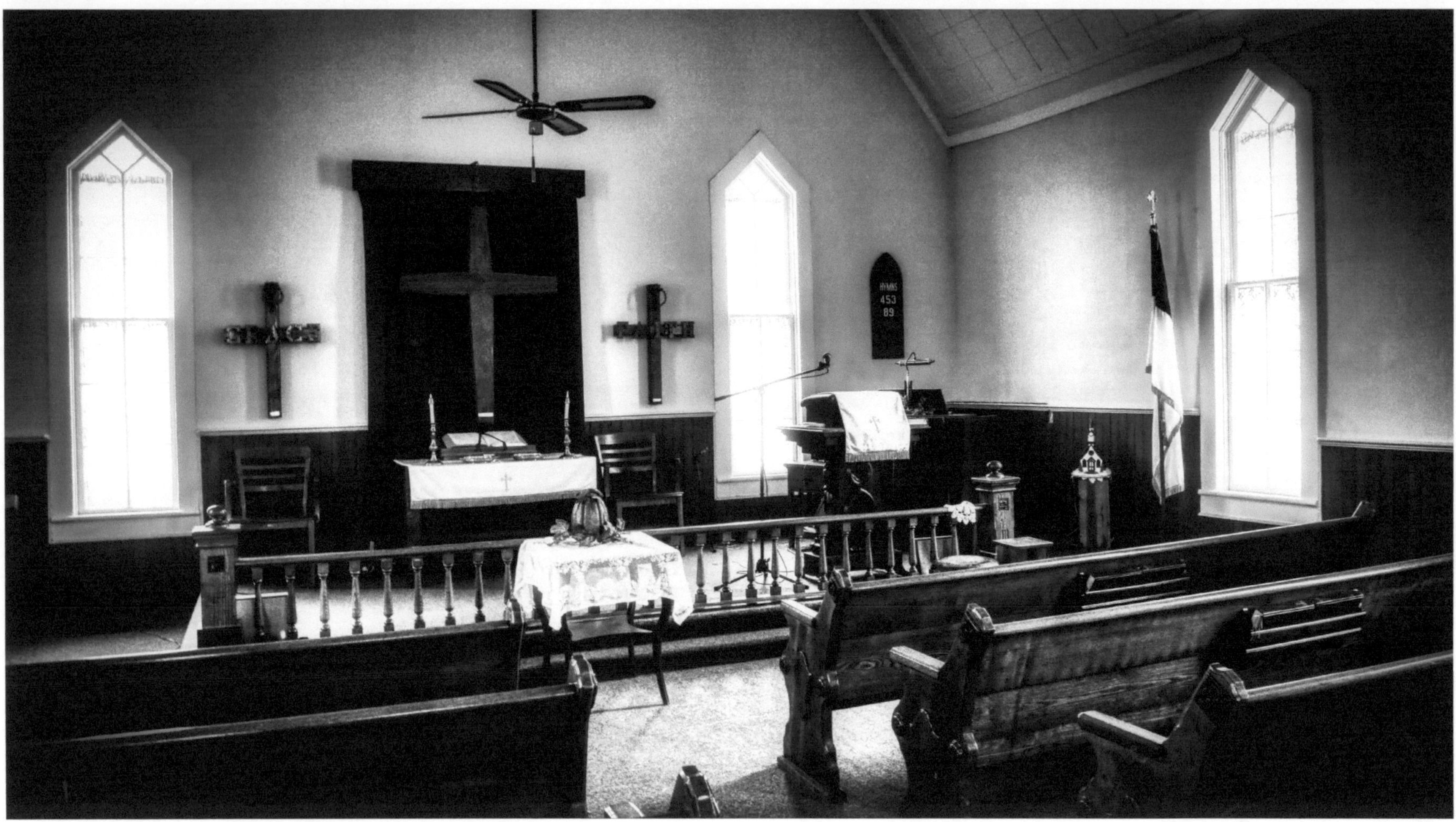

OKETO UNITED METHODIST CHURCH

Oketo, Kansas

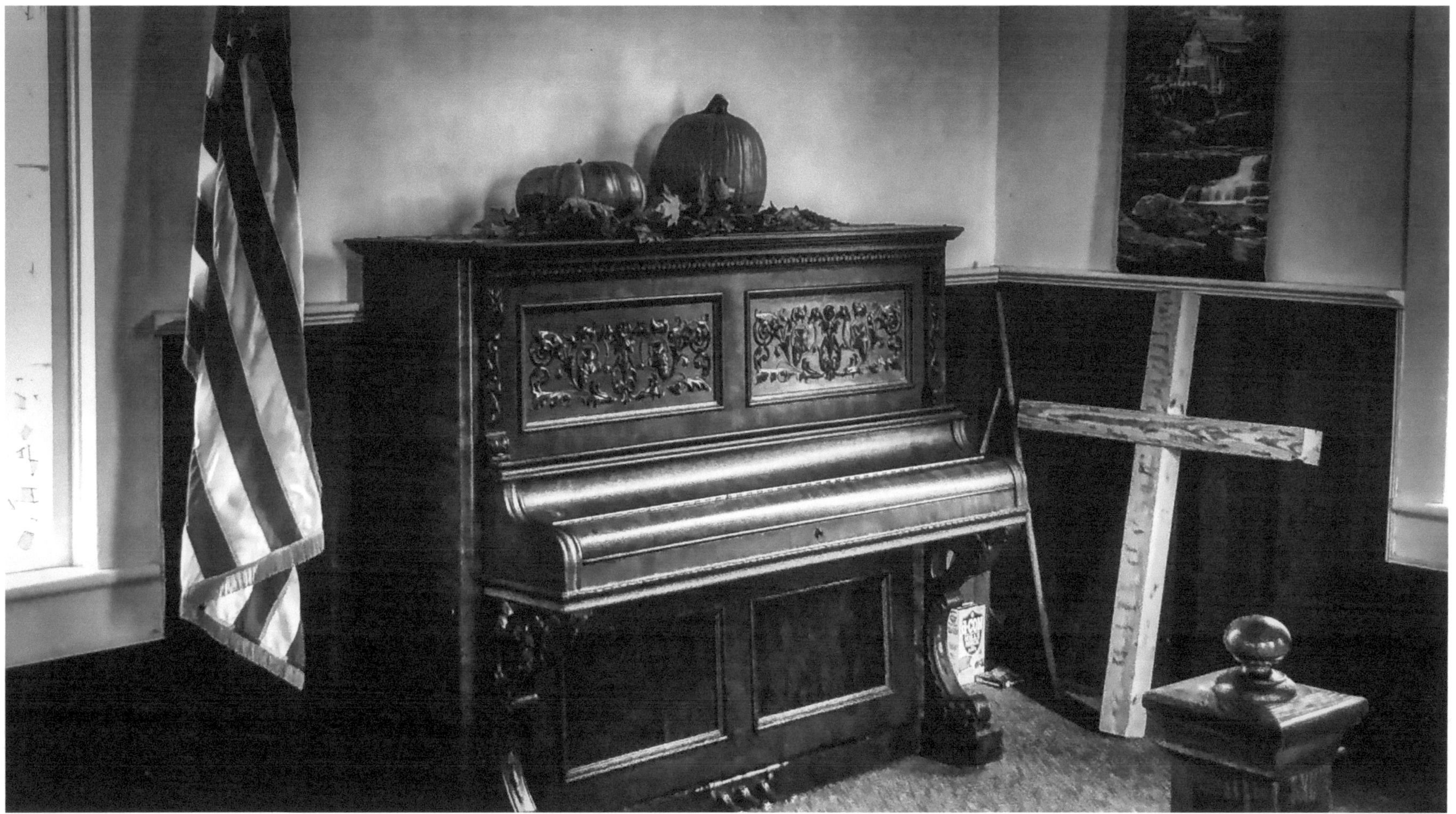

AXTELL UNITED METHODIST CHURCH

Axtell, Kansas

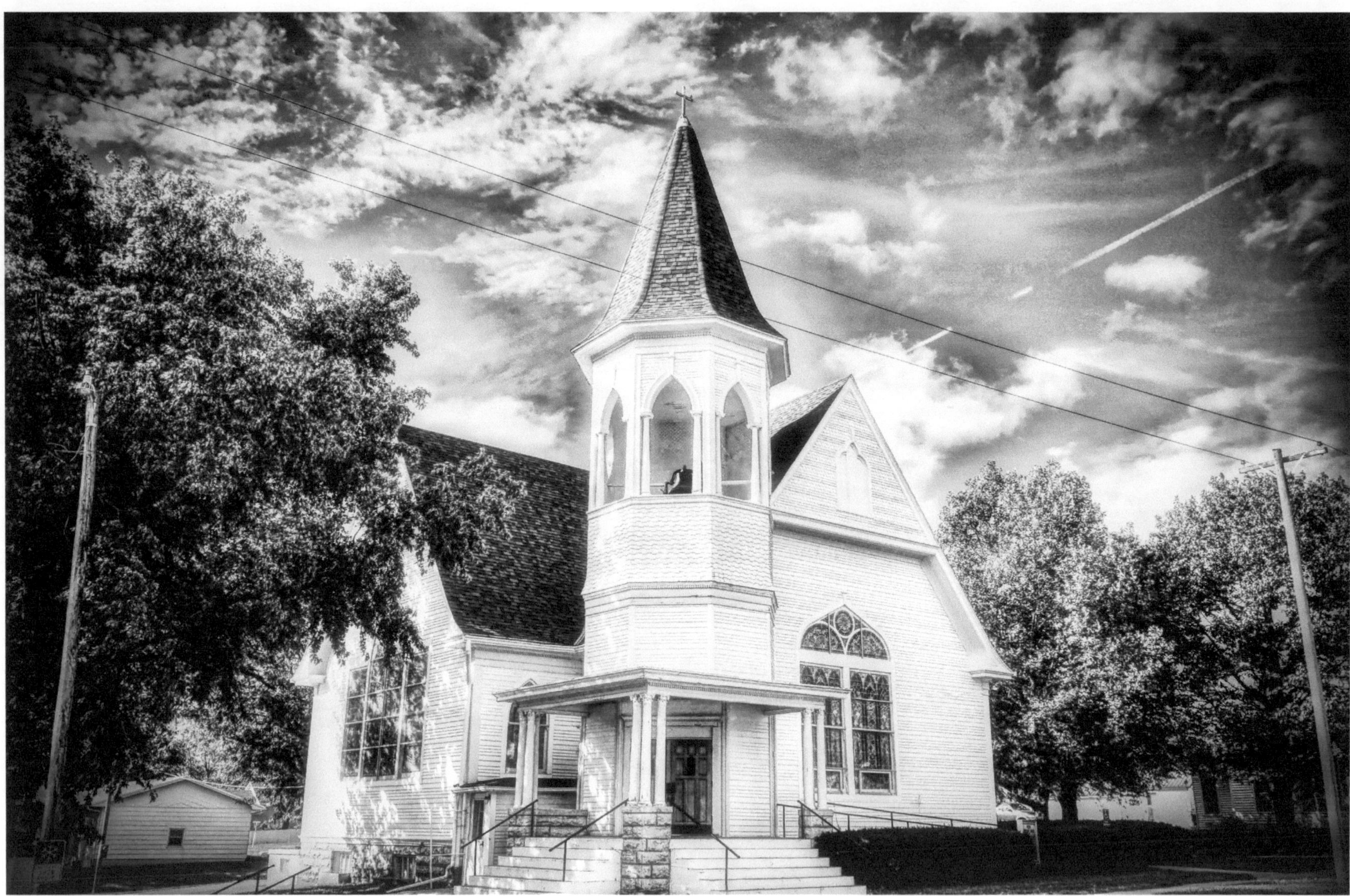

STANDING IN THIS LIGHT

1 CORINTHIANS 13 – (NRSV)

*12 For now we see in a mirror, dimly, but then
we will see face to face. Now I know only in part;
then I will know fully, even as I have been fully known.*

Rising up from the high prairie
Where gentle hills softly hold
A bell tower and steeple
Whitened with a shimmering
Light curving down from the sky
We are transformed in stages
Standing in this light
Upon these church steps
Bathed in a heavenly glow
Which seems so ethereal now
As if paradise has opened wide
And showered its benedictions
Upon the land and its kind
We have imagined something
New within this revered space
God's righteous reign present
Now and yet still to come
A Pentecostal fire burning
With an assurance well known

As the *Holy Spirit* kindles
In humanity a reconciling flame
Unafraid in our uncertainty
Across unpretentious years
And all of human history
What then after waiting
And being so long awake
In the beauty of this light
Where time's vastness dissolves
And our transformation
Comes so suddenly
In a fortunate undoing
An unending beingness
Where led so vibrantly
We come to know and are
Miraculously known
Moment by moment
By a greater Mystery
Flowing through creation

BEATTIE UNITED METHODIST CHURCH

Beattie, Kansas

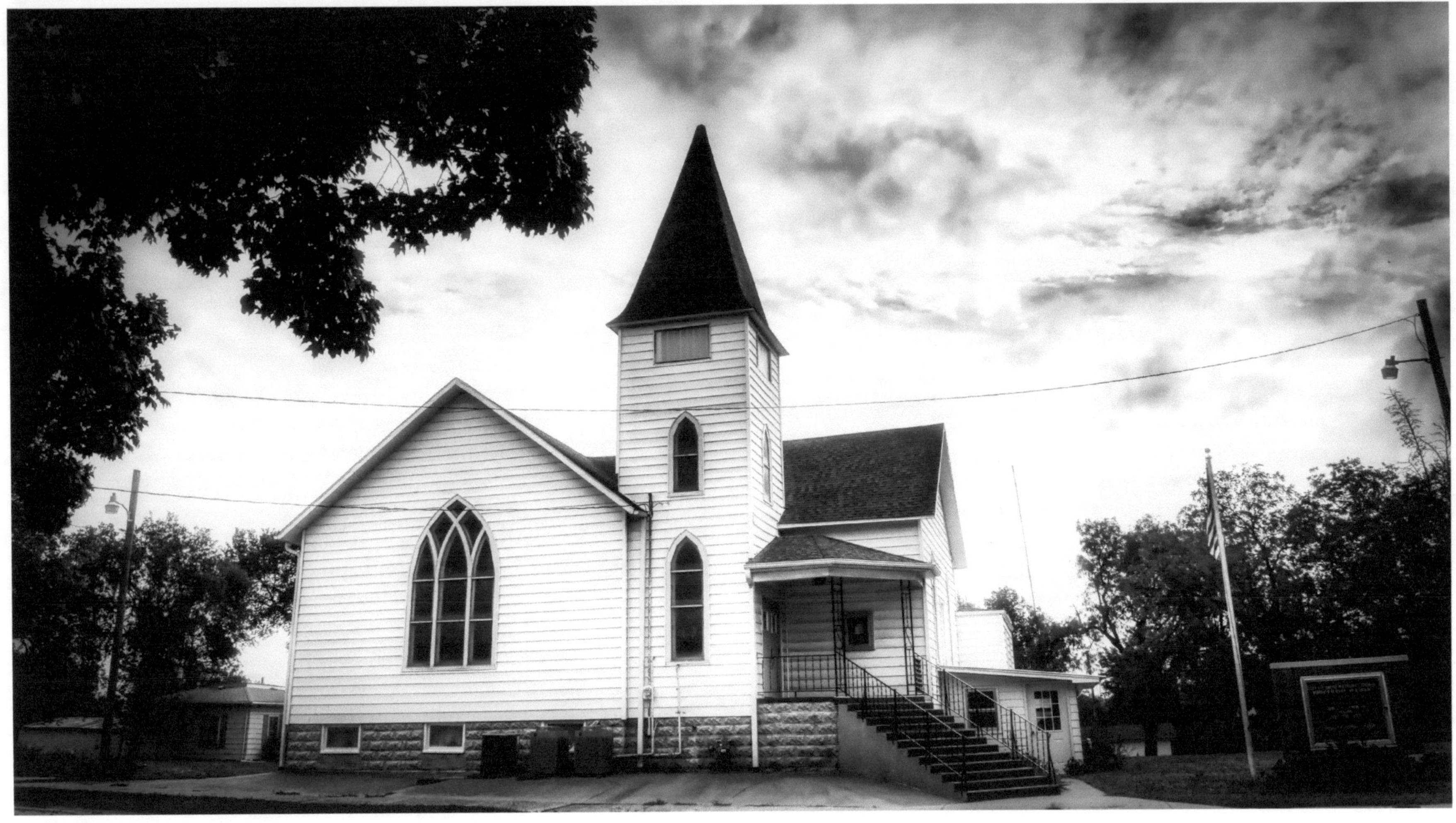

GATHER IN THIS LIGHT

ACTS 17:28-29 – (NRSV)

28 "For 'In him we live and move and have our being'; as even some of your own poets have said, 'For we too are his offspring.' 29 Since we are God's offspring, we ought not to think that the deity is like gold, or silver, or stone, an image formed by the art and imagination of mortals."

Let us gather together
In consecrated places where
We worship as one body
Where perpetual light
Pours from the spirit in
Infinite particles and waves
A divine *perichoresis*
Through which we dance
In a unity of wholeness
Vibrant in every living being
Known in a limitless
Mystery whose true name
Is concealed and waiting
For humanity to uncover
Let us wait in this light
Let us wait in the Lord
Where we may reconcile
Our darkness to become
Luminous in this time
As our stillness turns
With delight towards simple
Movement and then prayer
Drawn by these ancient rites
In forever known liturgical
Languages of faith and *praxis*
While the obscure dissolves
From chaos and possession
When the mind grows conscious
Once more of its lucid grace
Come one and all to adore
Here within these timid walls
By foot or horse and carriage
Or more modern means
In passages affluent in hope
A lovingkindness revealed
Progressing out from realms
Far beyond our mortal thoughts
Our intently measured words
Respire vibrantly in rectitude
In an emulation of angelic
Songs first sung in heaven
Our gratitude for creation
Caroled now once more
Let us make this paradise
Resonate here on earth
So invisibly disclosed

FRANKFORT UNITED METHODIST CHURCH

Frankfort, Kansas

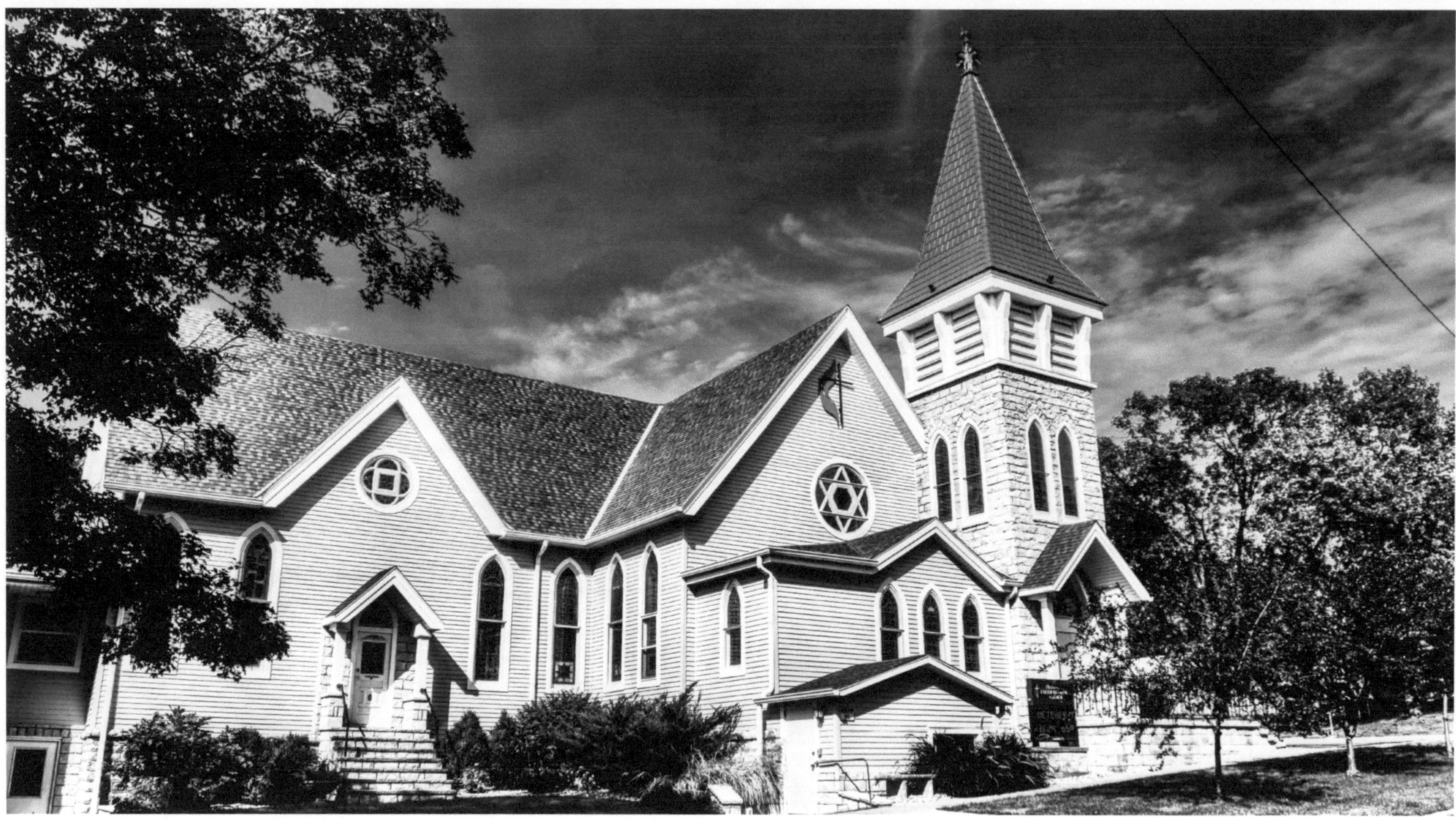

ENTERING IN

MATTHEW 11 – (AKJV)

28 Come unto me, all ye that labour and are heavy laden, and
I will Give you rest. 29 Take my yoke upon you, and learn of me;
for I am meek and lowly in heart: and ye shall find rest unto your souls.

Rest within our hearts
O Christ and take these
Burdens from us here

Teach us such a humility of
Spirit that we may easily take
your yoke upon us

To learn of your reign
Grant us that meekness
And lower the hurried

Expectations we seek
From life – to instead
Rest in you now

Enter into us – so that we may
In need repose here with you
Always and everywhere

As in these holy places which teach
Us to empty the self of conflict and
Confusion— to dwell in your light

THE OLD STONE CHURCH

Congregational Church – Maple Hill, Kansas

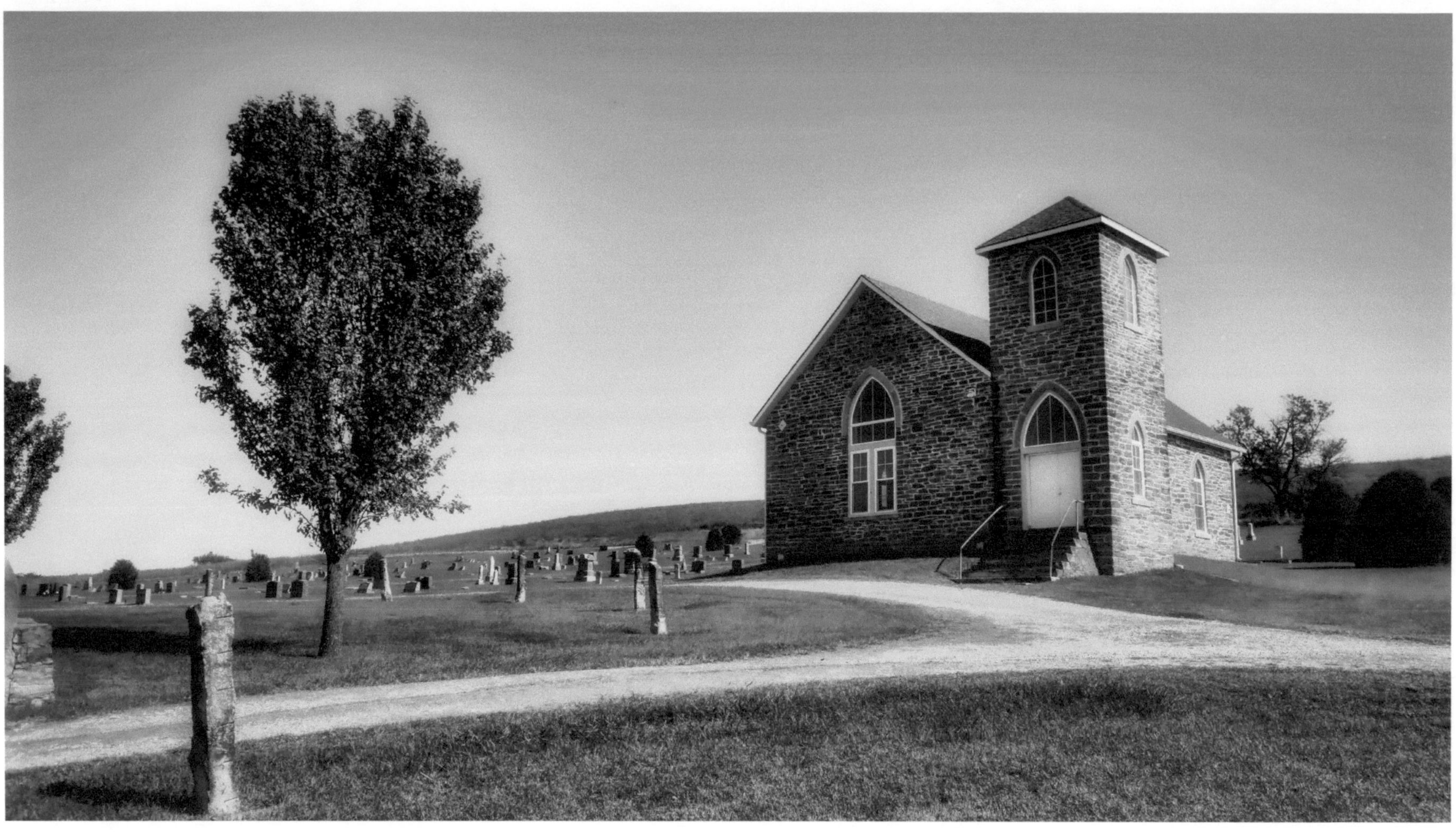

THE OLD STONE CHURCH

1 KINGS 6 – (KJV)

2 And the house which king Solomon built for the Lord, the length thereof was threescore cubits, and the breadth thereof twenty cubits, and the height thereof thirty cubits.

And the people dreamed
And strong hands gathered
To hew the stones and lift
Them high upon each other
Then they cut the timber
And shaped its form as one
To build this house of the Lord
Strong are the stone walls
Rising up from Bluestem Pastures
Across these Flint Hills
Hidden away in the fields
And farmland where crops
Were planted and are still
Now – even today
By the estimation of
Our naked eyes
The length thereof
May be close to fifty cubits
And the breadth thereof
Perhaps twenty cubits
And height thereof
Twenty-five cubits
And the church tower
Some thirty cubits high
And the windows formed
As narrow lights
Where inside walls
And beams perhaps
Of cedar made
Even King Solomon
In all his glory would
Clearly see how the Lord
Comes to dwell
Amongst his people
To make of them all
A people of God

FLINT HILLS
Tallgrass Prairie National Preserve

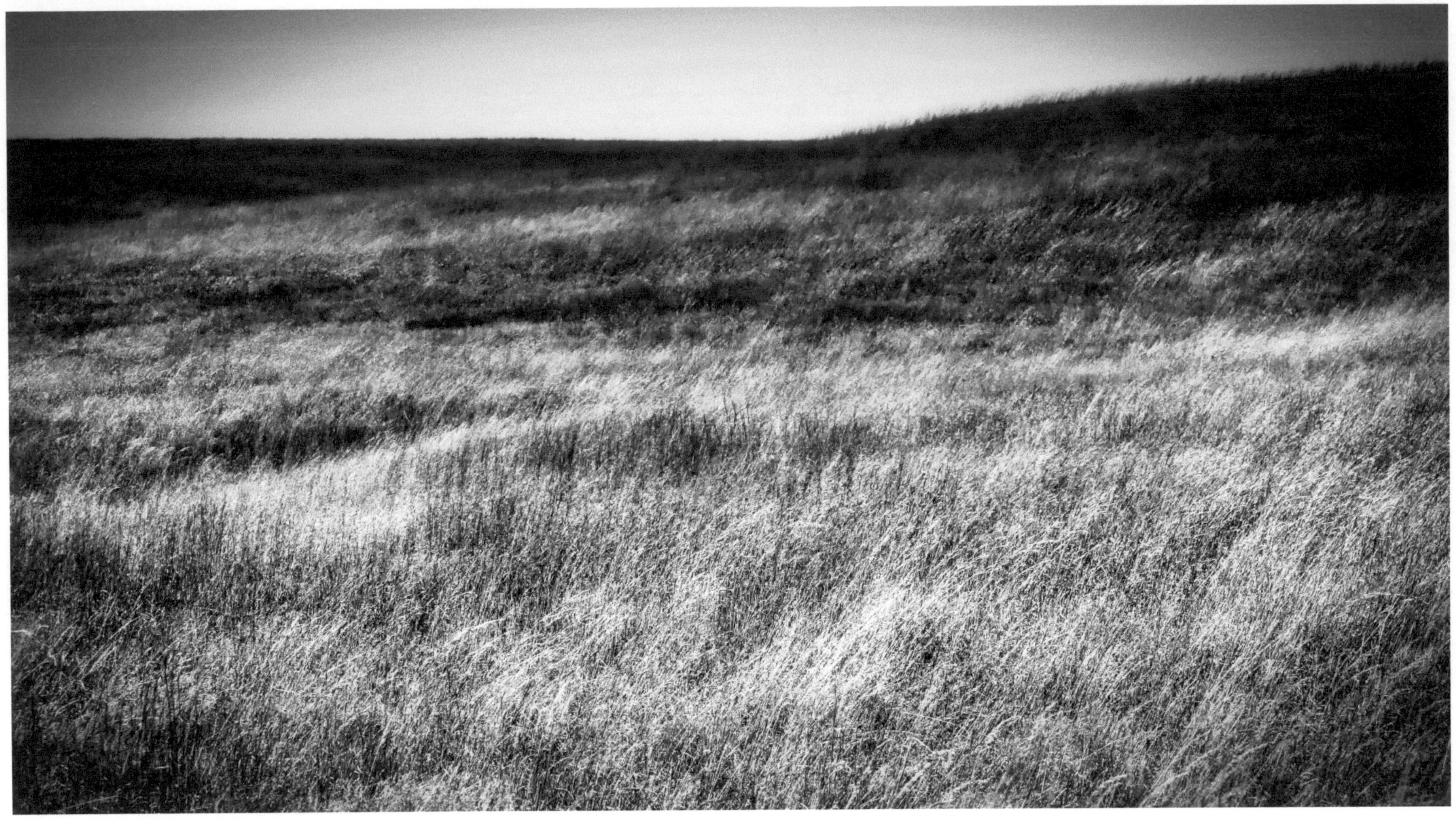

BLUESTEM PRAIRIE

12 A SONG OF CREATION – (BCP)
Benedicite, omnia opera Domini
II The Earth and its Creatures
Let the earth glorify the Lord,
praise him and highly exalt him for ever.
Glorify the Lord, O mountains and hills,
and all that grows upon the earth,
praise him and highly exalt him for ever.

Standing high amid curving sage-green
Bronze- and chestnut-colored hills before
An endless horizon where prairie sky
Meets prairie earth feels everlasting
Limitless – as if divinely formed
A world where no boundaries
Exist and all life arises in a soft
Harmony and gratitude woven together
In an eternal cycle we've always known
At the motionless point of its own turning
Where all earthly life is surrounded
By an unending light and grace
Creation blessed – where humanity
Waits and observes as witnesses
Learning from indigenous kind
Who walked so easy upon the land
To honor and guard it with kindness
Watching the many seasons unveil
The changing habits and passages
Of the Bison and Pronghorn Antelope
Whitetail Deer and Wapiti Elk
Where native wildlife flourishes
With an abundance
On acreages cherished
Migrating across landscapes
Sacred with hope to mark
A passing from one moment
To another in the movement
And motion of freed celestial bodies
In a joyful attendance of the light
Found here within this utter stillness
Where earth's formation springs forth
As a revelation of even flowing
Contours and a ground swell
From time's beginning where
Tallgrass and Bluestem Prairies
Arise as waves upon the verdant
Green hills and secret blue glens
Reflected on the eye's inner surface
From God's eternal vision

FLINT HILLS

Tallgrass Prairie National Preserve

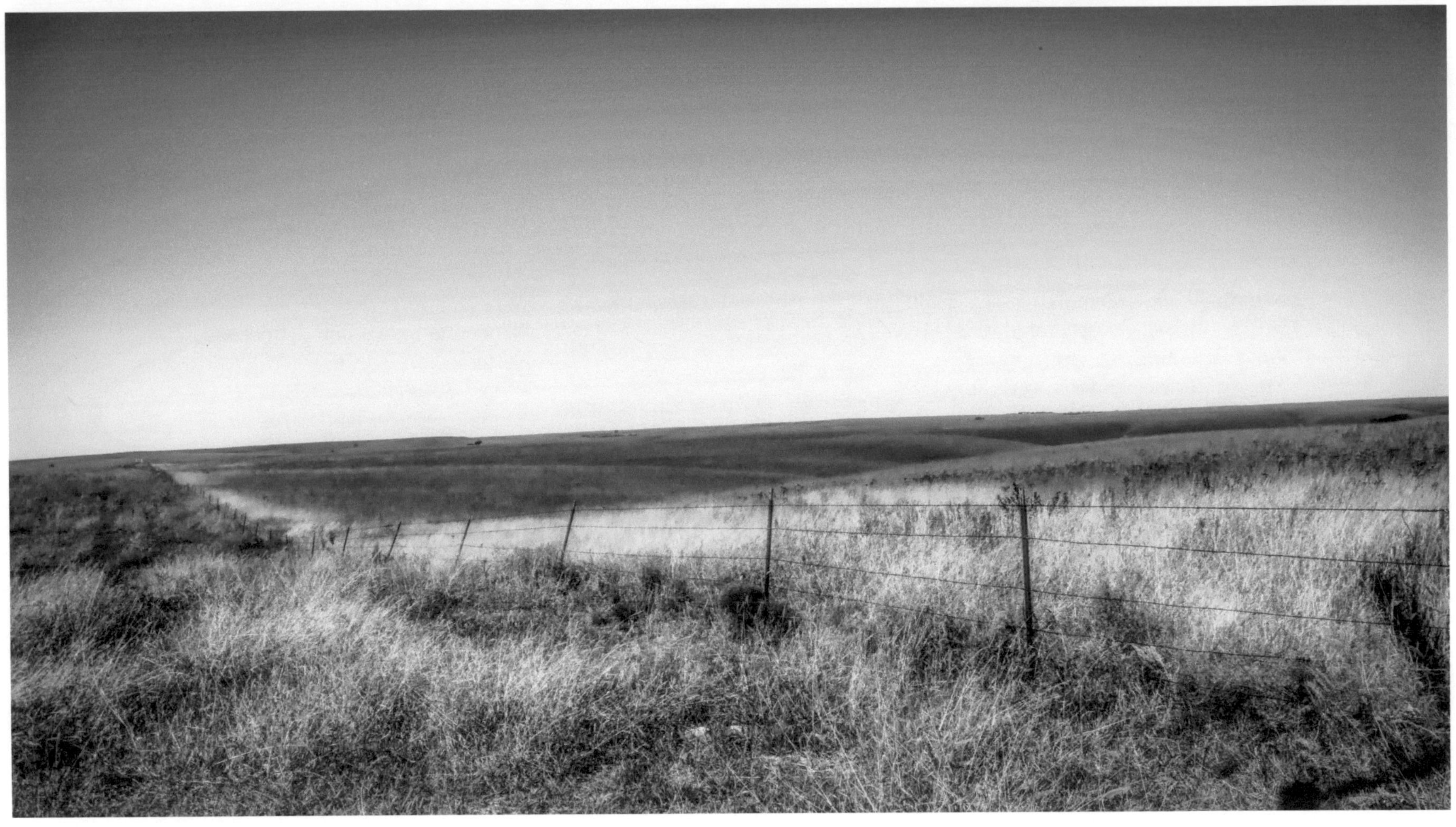

FLINT HILLS

Tallgrass Prairie National Preserve

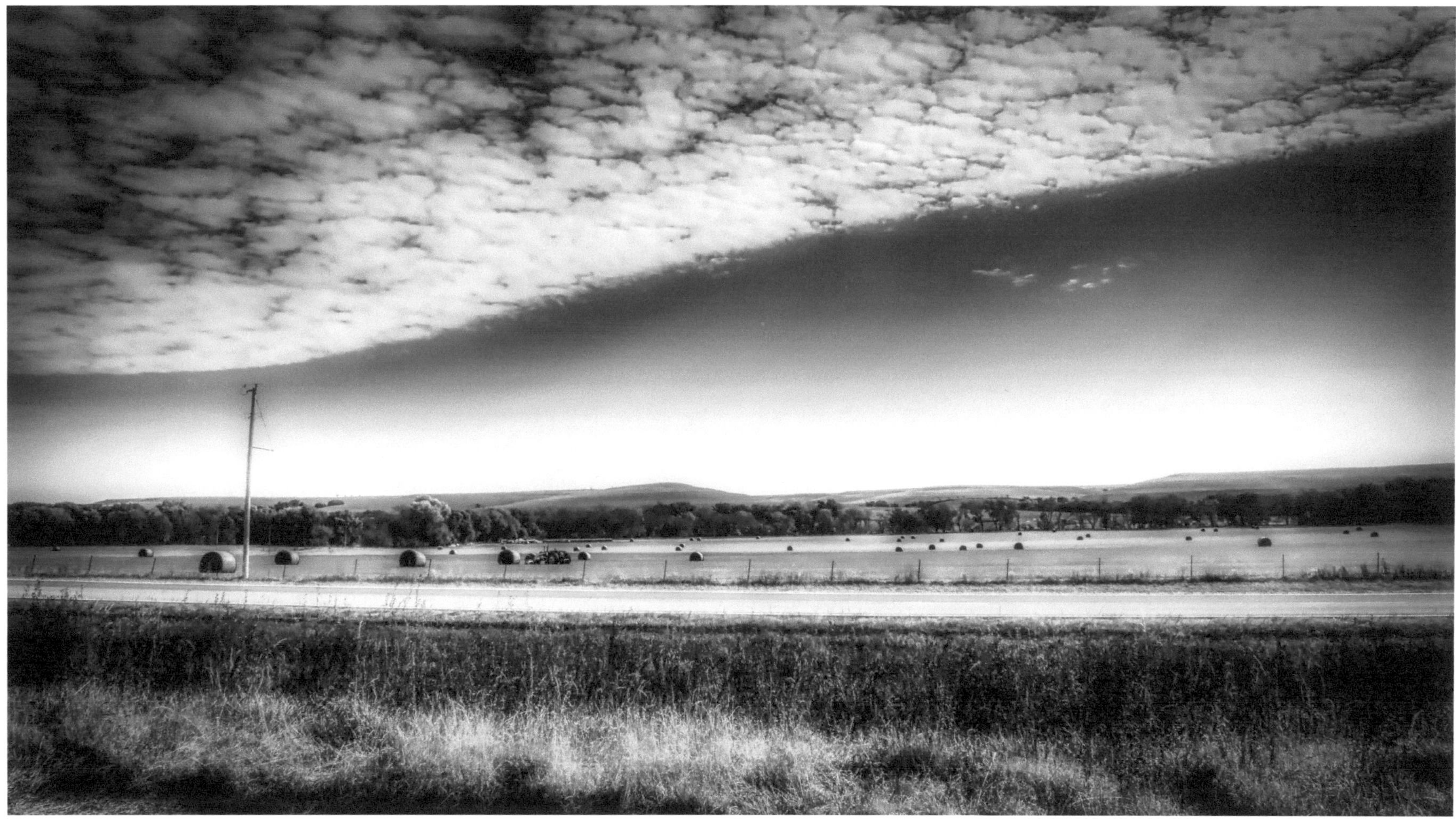

FLINT HILLS – HORSES
South of Matfield Green, Kansas

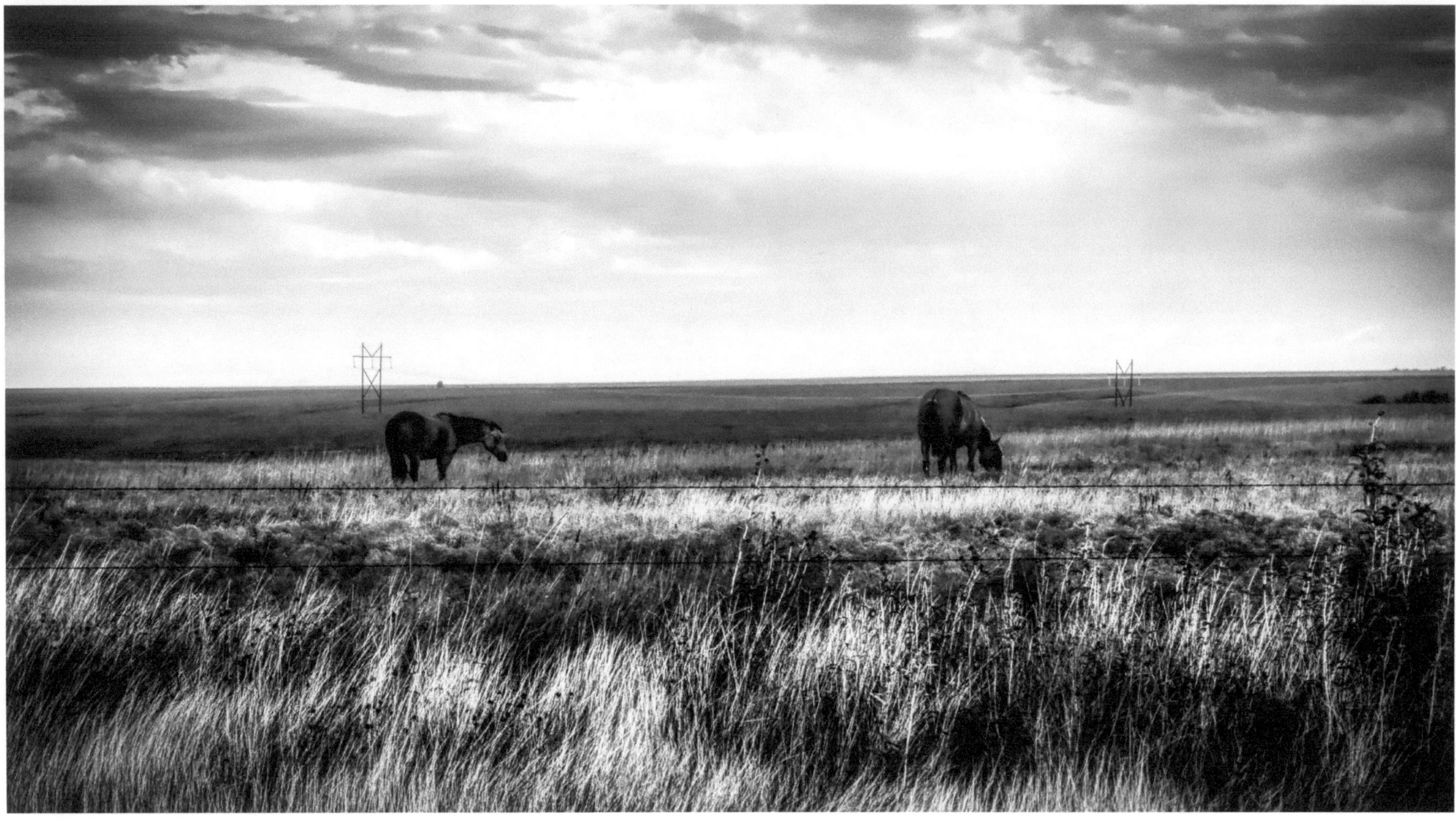

DIVINE AMAZEMENT

ACTS 17 – (NRSV)

28 "For 'In him we live and move and have our being'; as even some of your own poets have said, 'For we too are his offspring.'"

This is how it begins
With the wild wind blowing
Cold and fierce across our face
And the air rushing toward us

Running with a grander abandonment
Horses prancing and dancing together
Under wide-ranging prairie sky and earth
Nostrils flaring open and breathing

In with a single full breath
Followed by another – the unbound
Sense of freedom found in the strong
Movement of muscle bone and hooves

Soaring across the high plains
Barely touching the ground
With a greater vision and flight
In a divine amazement

Where we see the world anew
As it really is – if we will
Only embrace a fuller vision
This is the Glory of God

Reflected in and with
And through all living things
Upon the earth – this no mystery
It is not even a miracle

It is simply what is – creation
It is seeing clearly through
Newborn eyes – once more
As if for the first time

We are that child or the colt
Born under brilliant white stars
As midnight crosses the land
Gamboling playfully – intuitive

Knowing who we are amid greater
Graces – where we come to know
God is more than mortals may imagine
God is the one radiance

That pervades all things
Of all faiths – the one in whom
We live and move
And have our being

FLINT HILLS – BISON

Tallgrass Prairie National Preserve

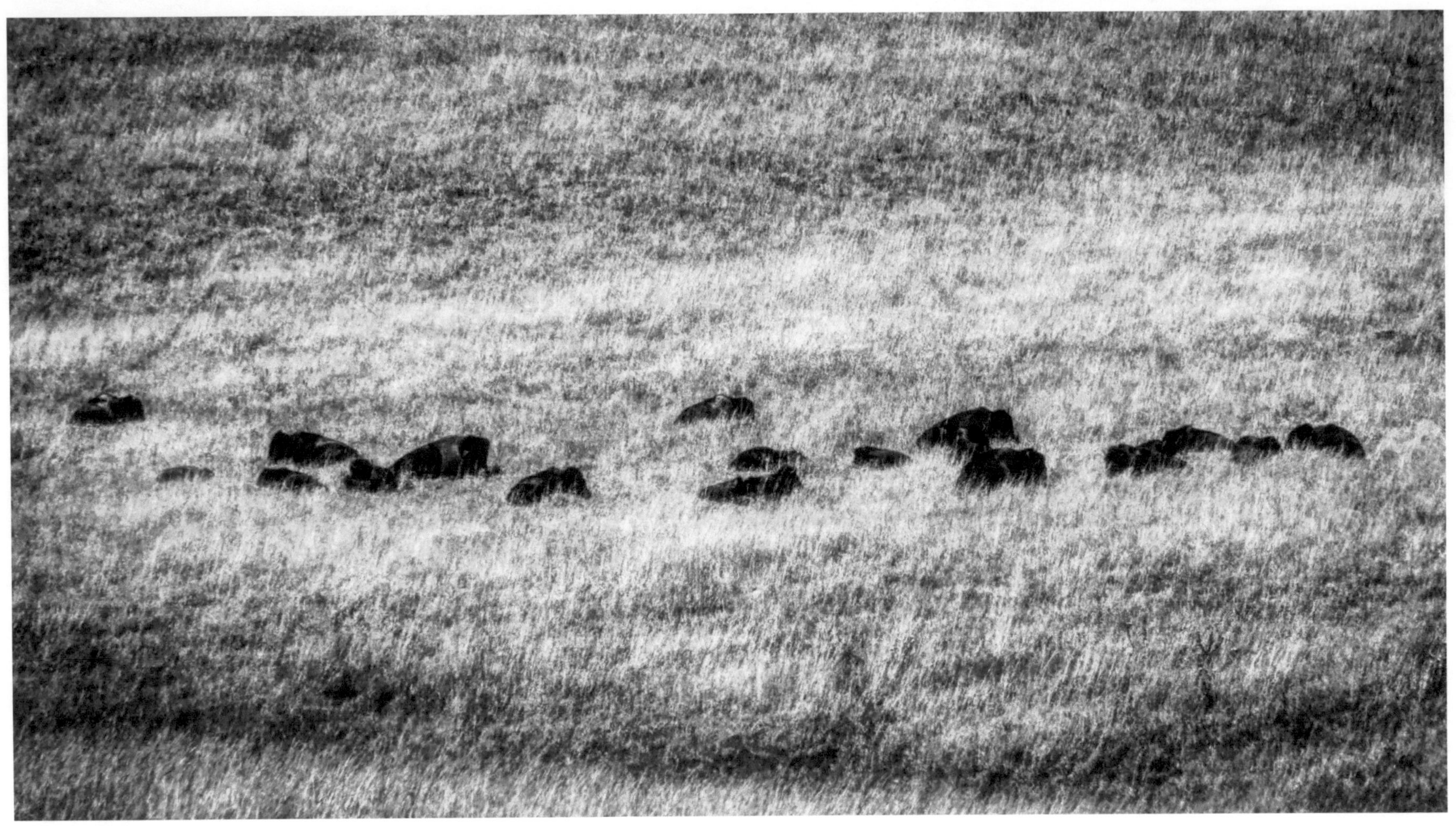

FLINT HILLS – CLOUDS
South of Matfield Green, Kansas

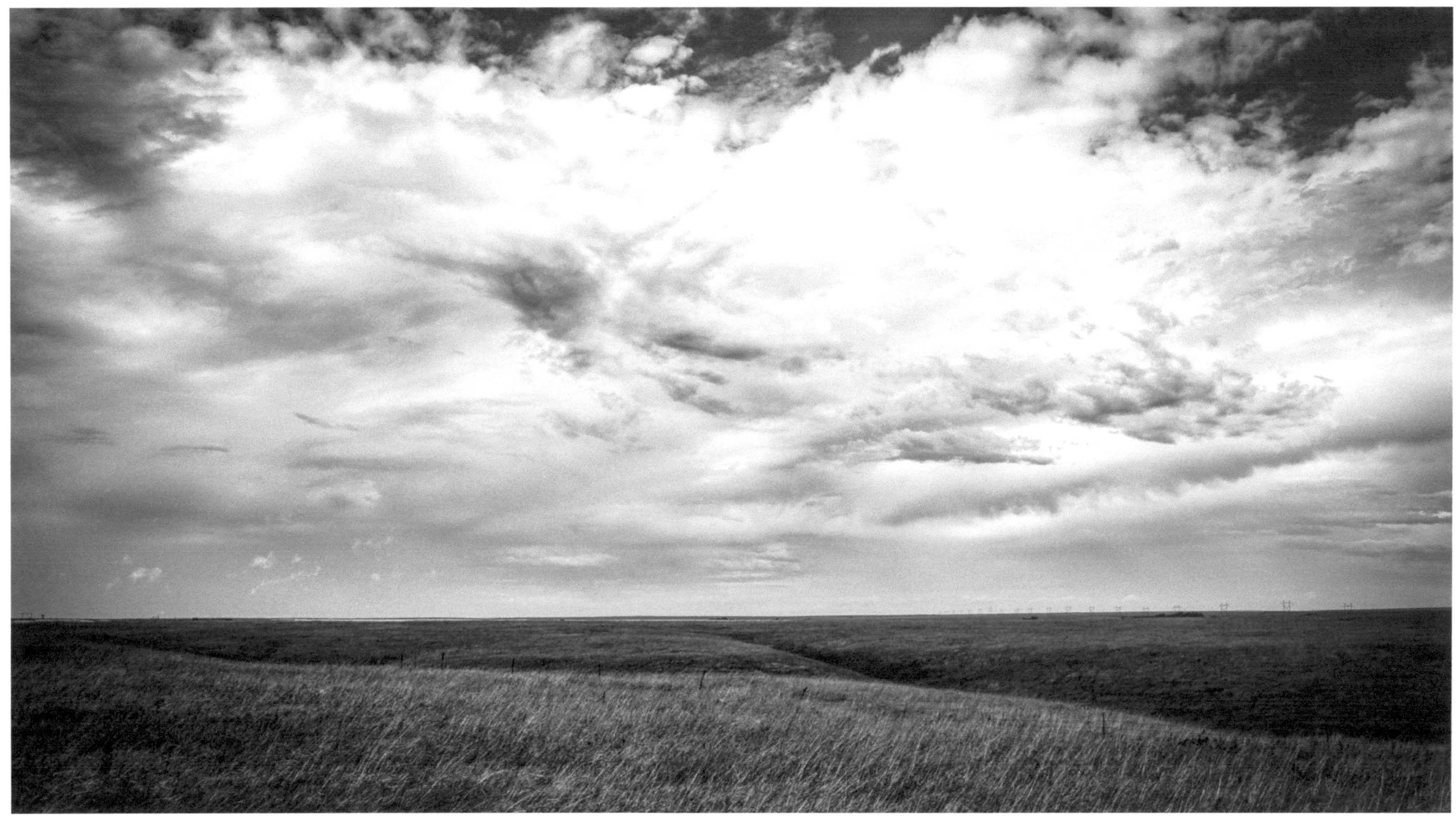

FLINT HILLS – STONE WALL

South of Alma, Kansas

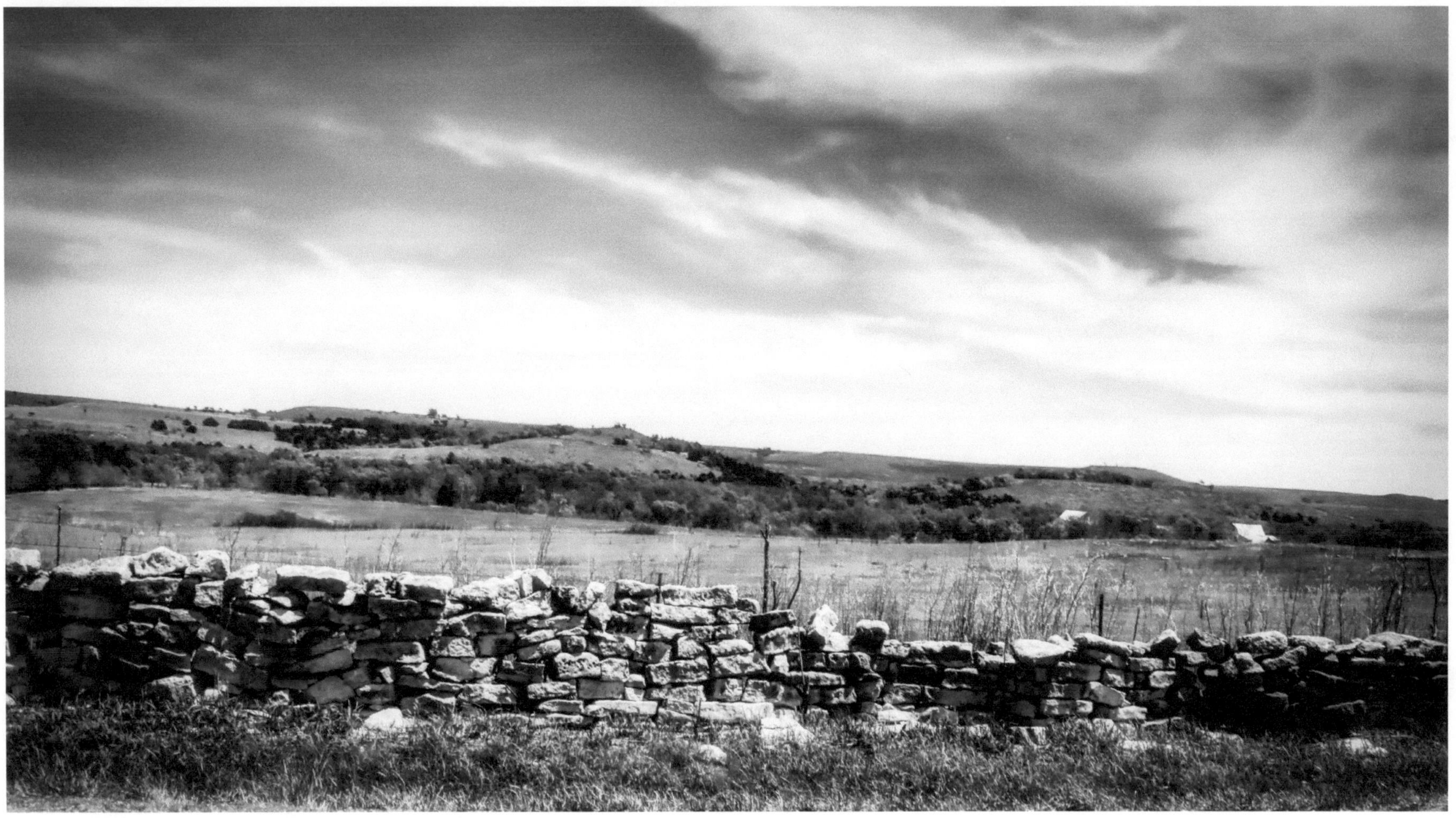

FLINT HILLS – OLD CORRAL

North of the Tallgrass Prairie National Preserve

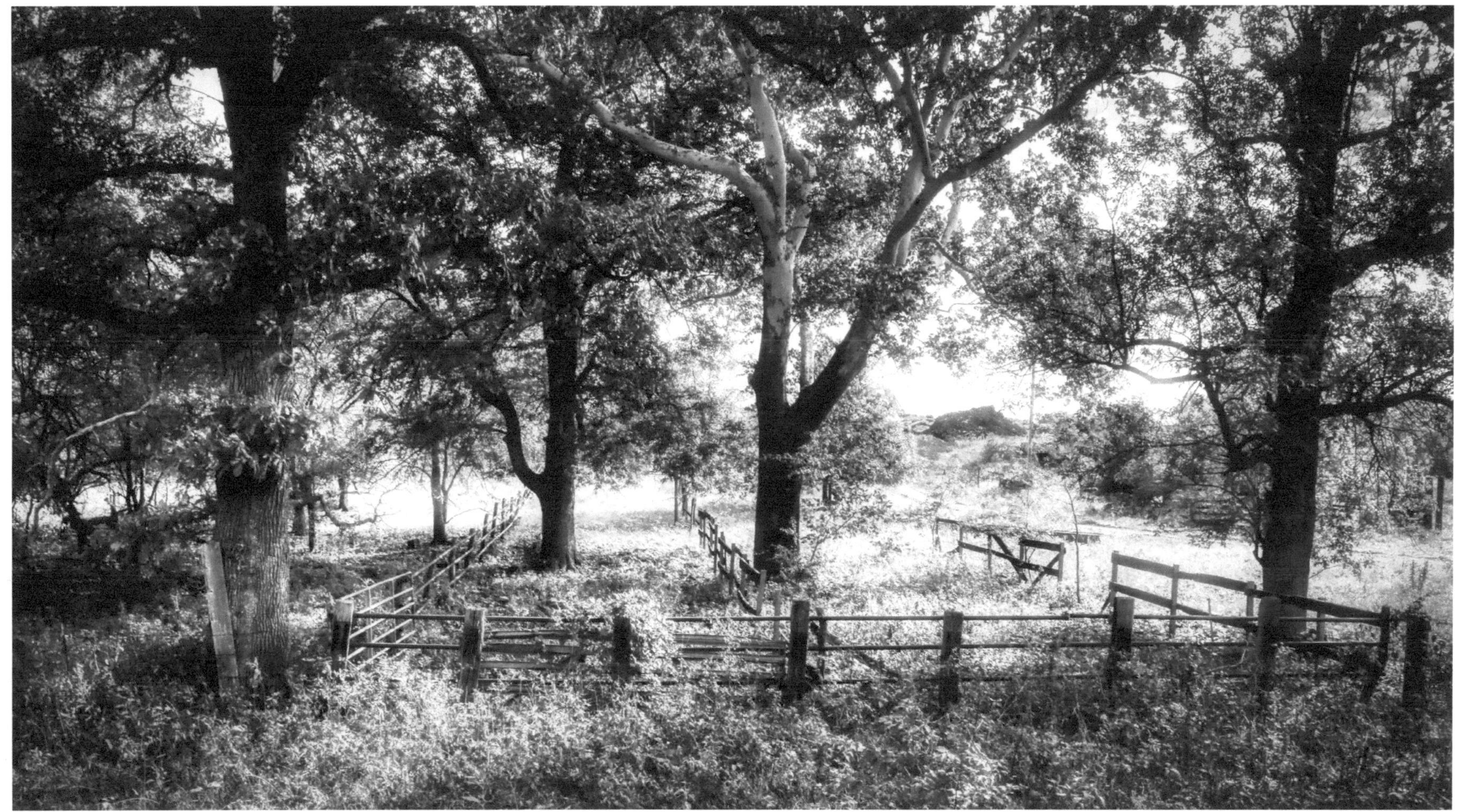

FLINT HILLS – LASSO & TALLGRASS SHEAF

Tallgrass Prairie National Preserve

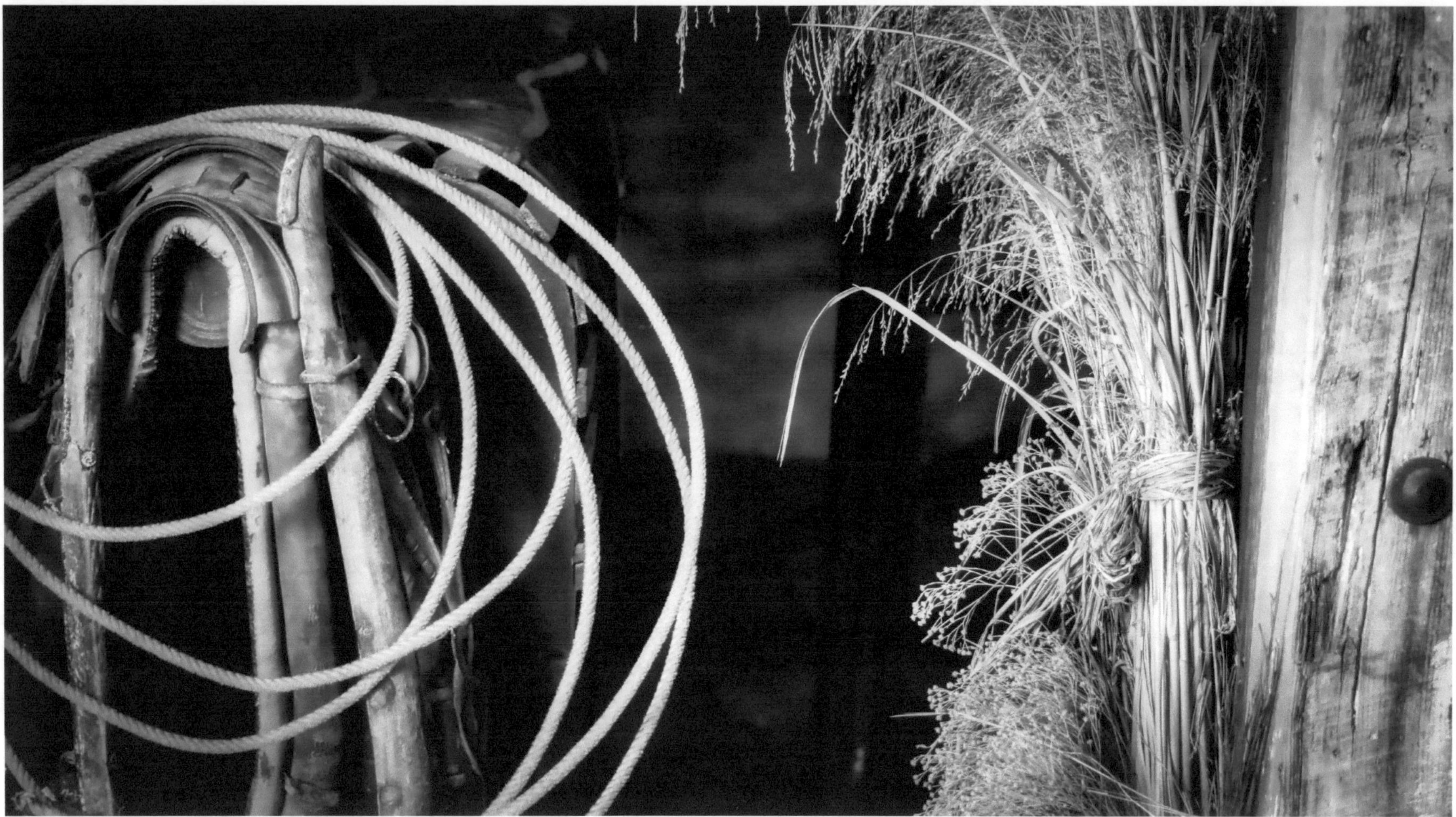

FLINT HILLS – FOX CREEK SCHOOLHOUSE

Tallgrass Prairie National Preserve

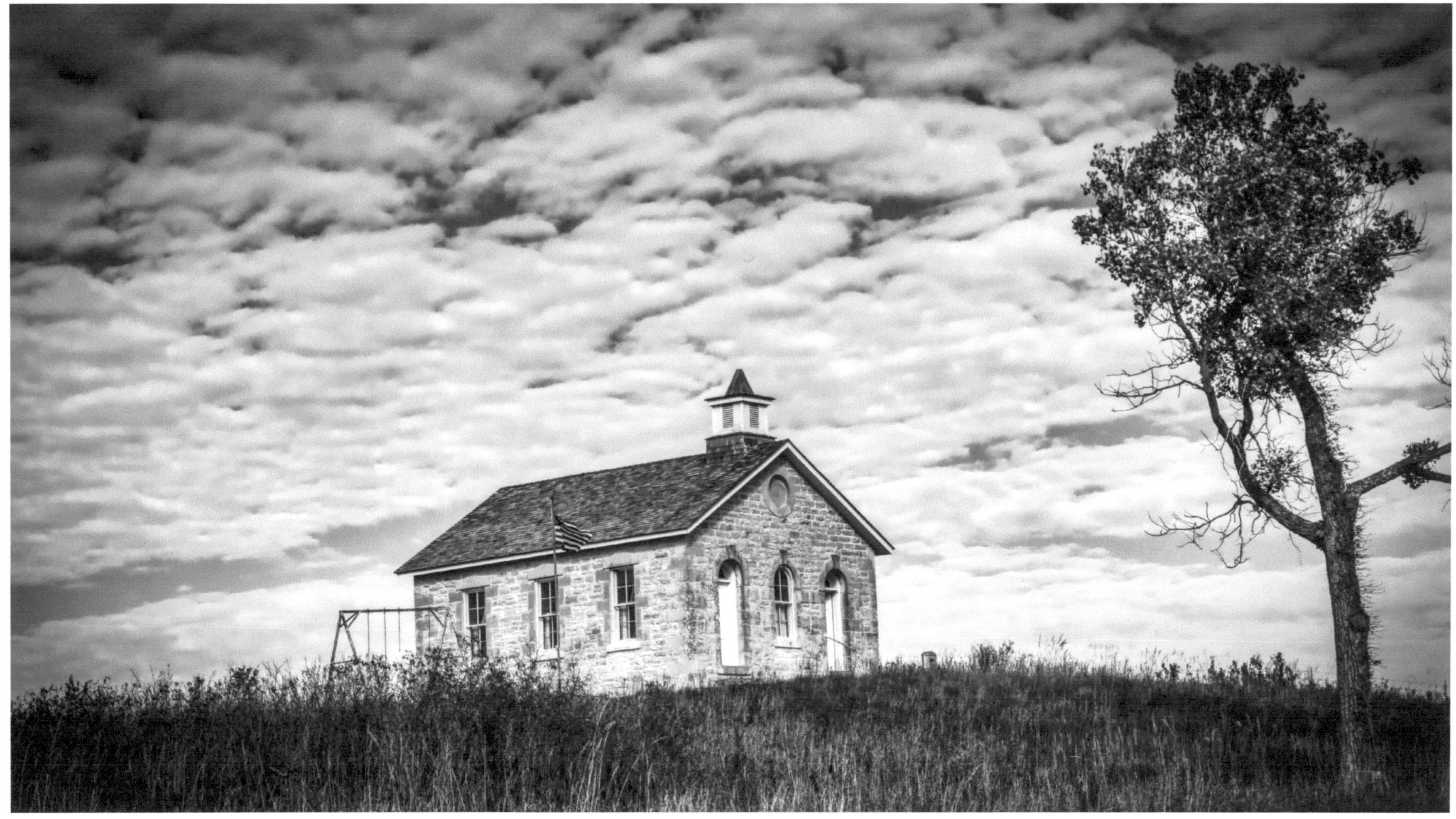

A Pilgrimage of Churches

The Great Plains

Houston—Coastal Plains

PSALM 100 *Jubilate Deo*

1 Be joyful in the Lord, all you lands;
serve the Lord with gladness
and come before his presence with a song.

2 Know this: The Lord himself is God;
he himself has made us, and we are his;
we are his people and the sheep of his pasture.

3 Enter his gates with thanksgiving;
go into his courts with praise;
give thanks to him and call upon his Name.

4 For the Lord is good;
his mercy is everlasting;
and his faithfulness endures from age to age.

TRINITY EPISCOPAL CHURCH

Midtown Houston, Texas

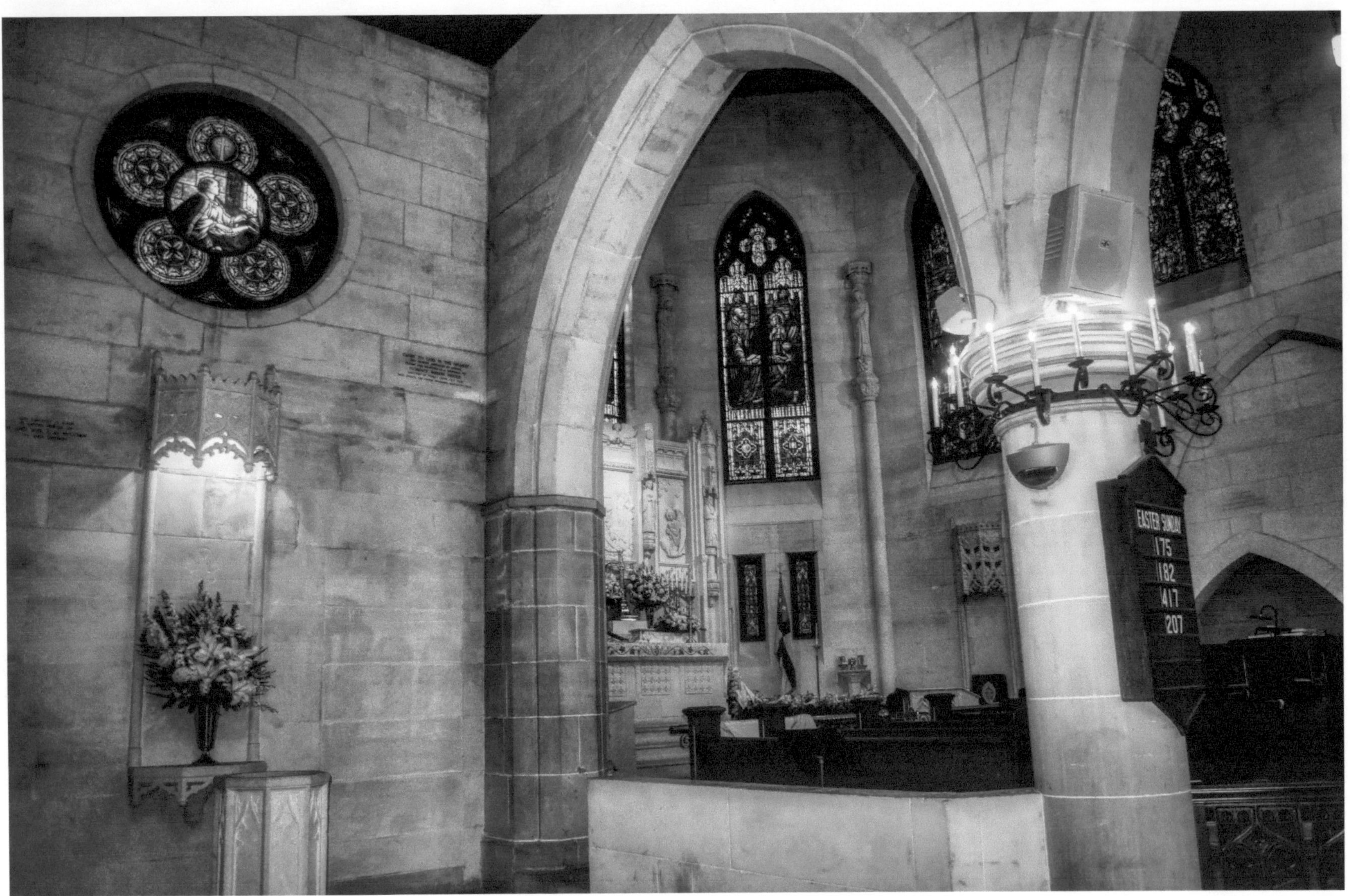

THANKSGIVING PRAISES

PSALM 95 Venite, exultemus

1 Come, let us sing to the Lord;
let us shout for joy to the Rock of our salvation.
2 Let us come before his presence with thanksgiving
and raise a loud shout to him with psalms.

Another year returns
In Thanksgiving
For all the times with you
When I was never alone
You were always there
It seems now
Even before the time
We knew one another
As if waiting for the
Next unhurried breath
To come without
Anxiousness in the certain
Knowledge of one another
Across immeasurable
Distances arising from
The vast emptiness
Of universal space
Where time stops

And then flows endlessly
Which no human being
Wholly understands
Even as one generation
Folds into another
Even as we move
Far beyond the little
That we do know
In this confusing
Here and now
Beyond all human
Memory yet to come
This is our time together
To bless and share
A greater Thanksgiving
Of faith and practice
Arising from the
Mystery of creation

TRINITY EPISCOPAL CHURCH
Midtown Houston, Texas

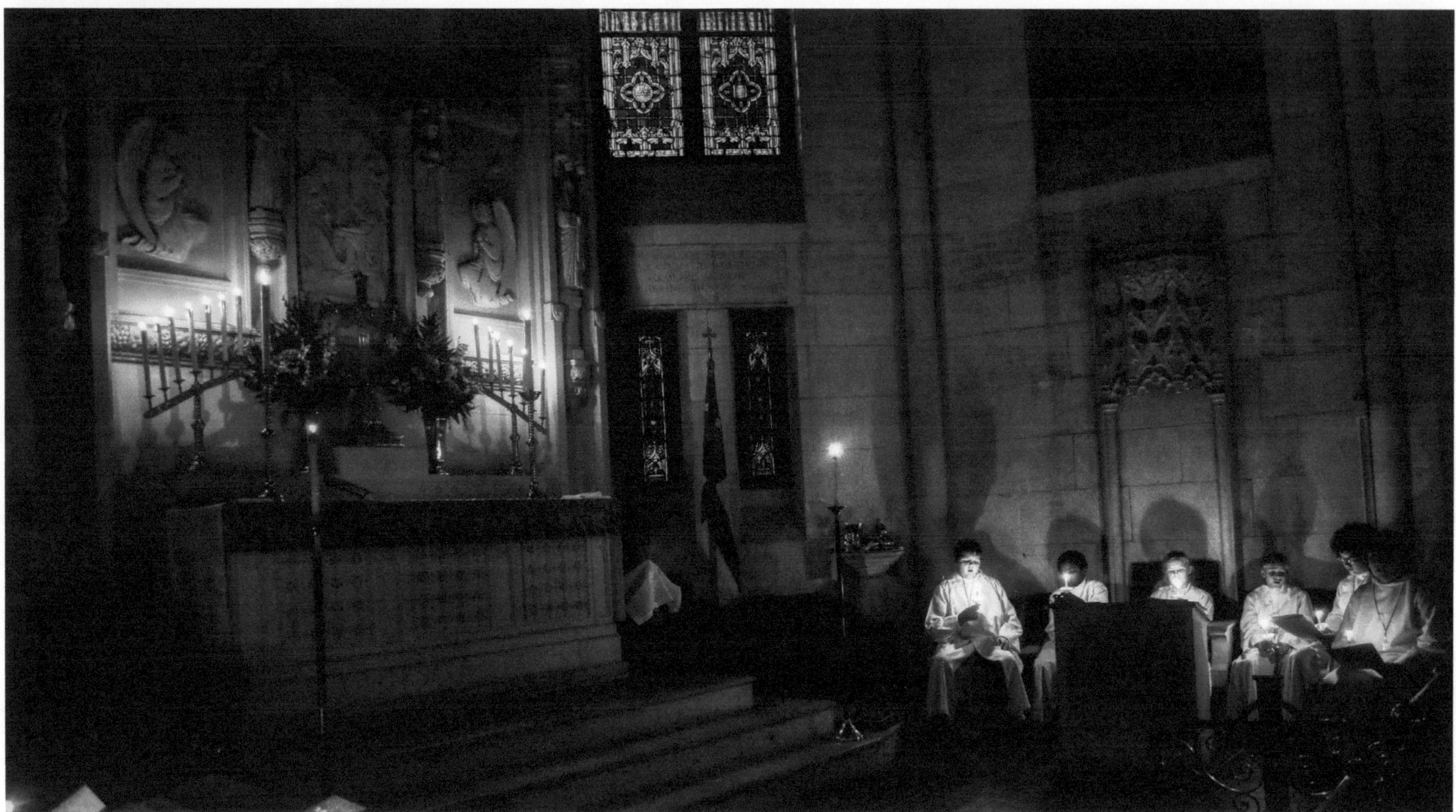

TRINITY ACOLYTES

LUKE 2 – (NRSV)

8 In that region there were shepherds living in the fields, keeping watch
over their flock by night. 9 Then an angel of the Lord stood before them,
and the glory of the Lord shone around them, and they were terrified.
10 But the angel said to them, "Do not be afraid; for see–I am bringing
you good news of great joy for all the people: 11 to you is born this day
in the city of David a Savior, who is the Messiah, the Lord."

There are always angels
Dwelling amongst us
Hidden often in plain sight
In a light reflecting off their faces
As acolytes honor a newborn
Child upon this Christmas Eve
O Lord bless us as we move
In silence towards a manger
Guarded by ox and ass
Humble and mute witnesses
Longing to know the birth of God's
Love within the world
Longing to see the Christ child
Coming to us in a fuller

Anticipation — unhurried
Now within this moment
Of our own rebirth
As we stumble together
Towards Bethlehem this night
Seeking a new creation
For the old one is gone
And the one new is here
Now in this place
In the open hearts of
All humankind
Silent this night
In a light breaking
Upon the altar cross

TRINITY EPISCOPAL CHURCH

Midtown Houston, Texas

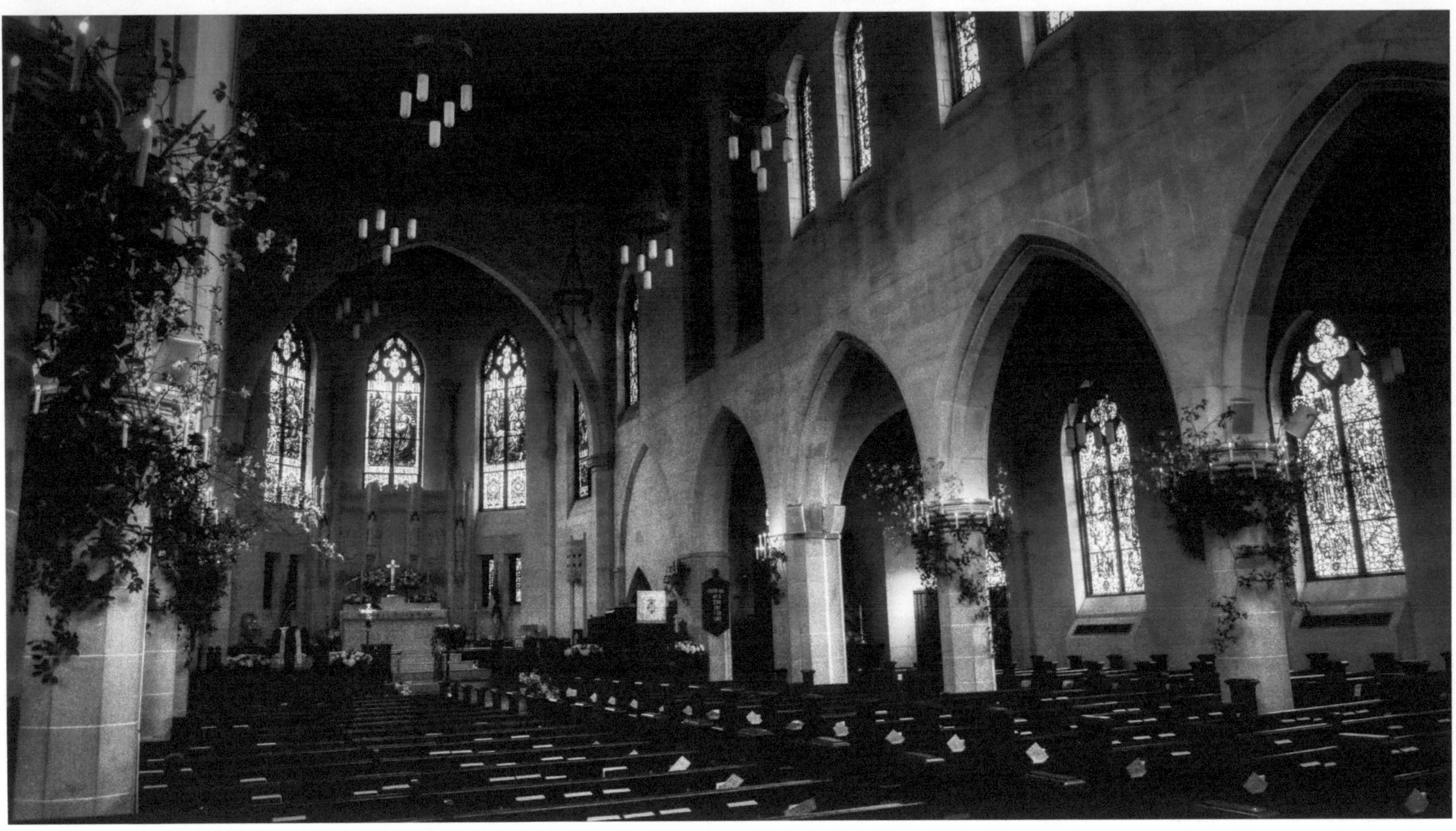

HALLELUJAHS

LUKE 2 – (NRSV)

13 And suddenly there was with the angel a multitude of the heavenly host,
praising God and saying,
14 "Glory to God in the highest heaven,
and on earth peace among those whom he favors!"

Jesus, we're going to take
Our time this year
And not rush through
This season of Advent
Or of Christmas
For that matter
Help us to empty
Ourselves in this
Kenosis of faith
Cloaking our minds
In a simple humility
We'll be happy
To play the parts of the
Magi or the little shepherd boy
Or imitate the humility
Of the ox and ass
We'll wait for you here
In the stable that
Mary and Joseph found
Because there was no place
For them in the inn
We'll sing hallelujahs
Without end
As the Archangels
And Angels did
When you were born
Into the world to heal
Our enmity and brokenness

TRINITY EPISCOPAL CHURCH
Midtown Houston, Texas

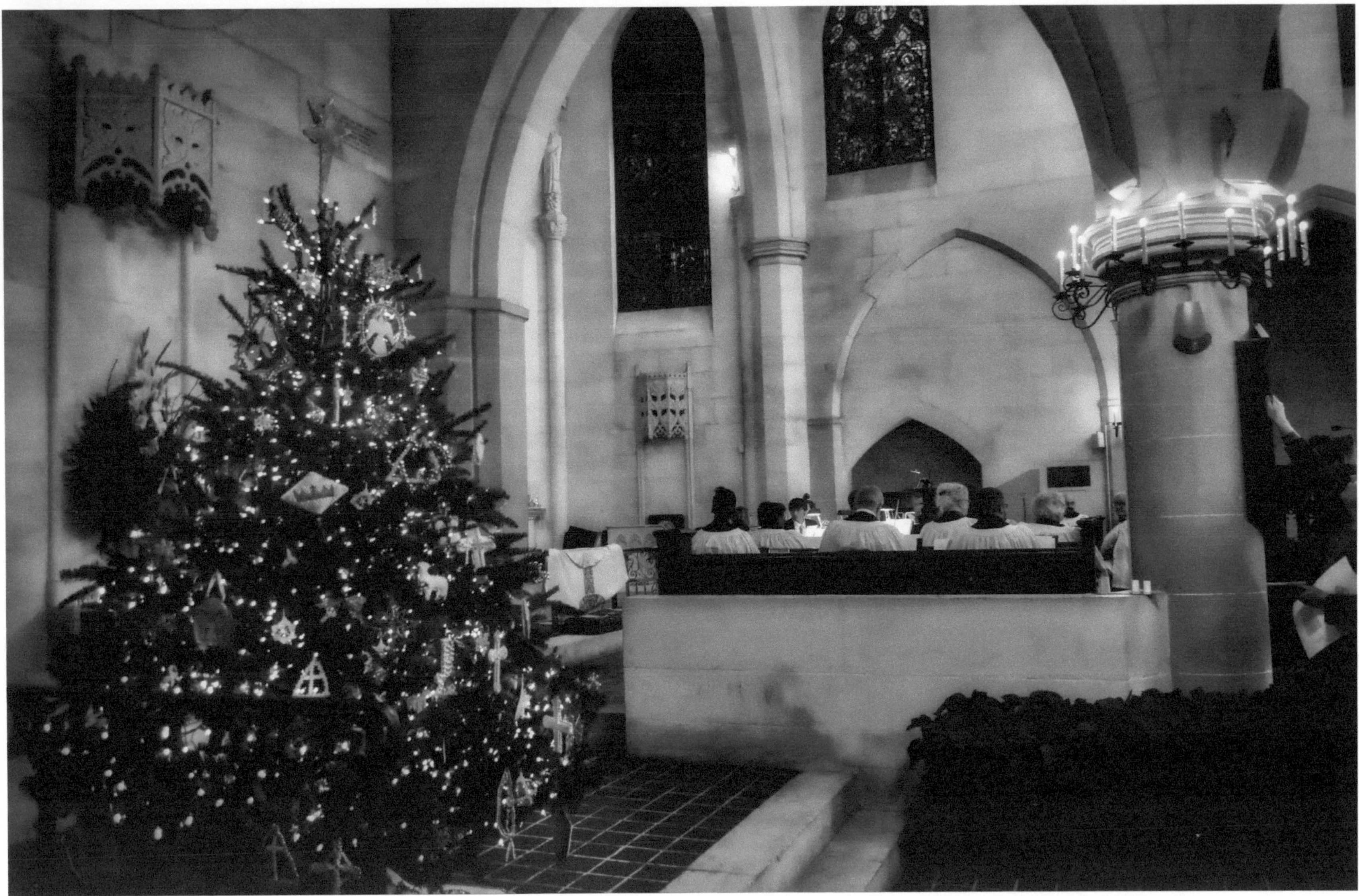

UPON THIS EVE

LUKE 2 – (NRSV)

10 But the angel said to them, "Do not be afraid; for see–I am bringing you good news of great joy for all the people: 11 to you is born this day in the city of David a Savior, who is the Messiah, the Lord."

In the stillness of this night
In a memory and thought
We cannot turn from now
Humankind celebrates
A child bedded in straw
A mother beside him
A father – both heavenly
And earthly watching over
A simple manger with a hope
For the whole world
In a light shining down
From a place above
We cannot quite see
Or believe at first
And yet – it is true
Upon this eve
In the holiness
We find within this night
The world is transformed
And we each become
A new creation
Even when we yet
Do not know
Or cannot see how
It is timeless
And eternal

GREATER PLEASANT HILL MISSIONARY BAPTIST CHURCH

Houston, Texas – Greater Heights Neighborhood

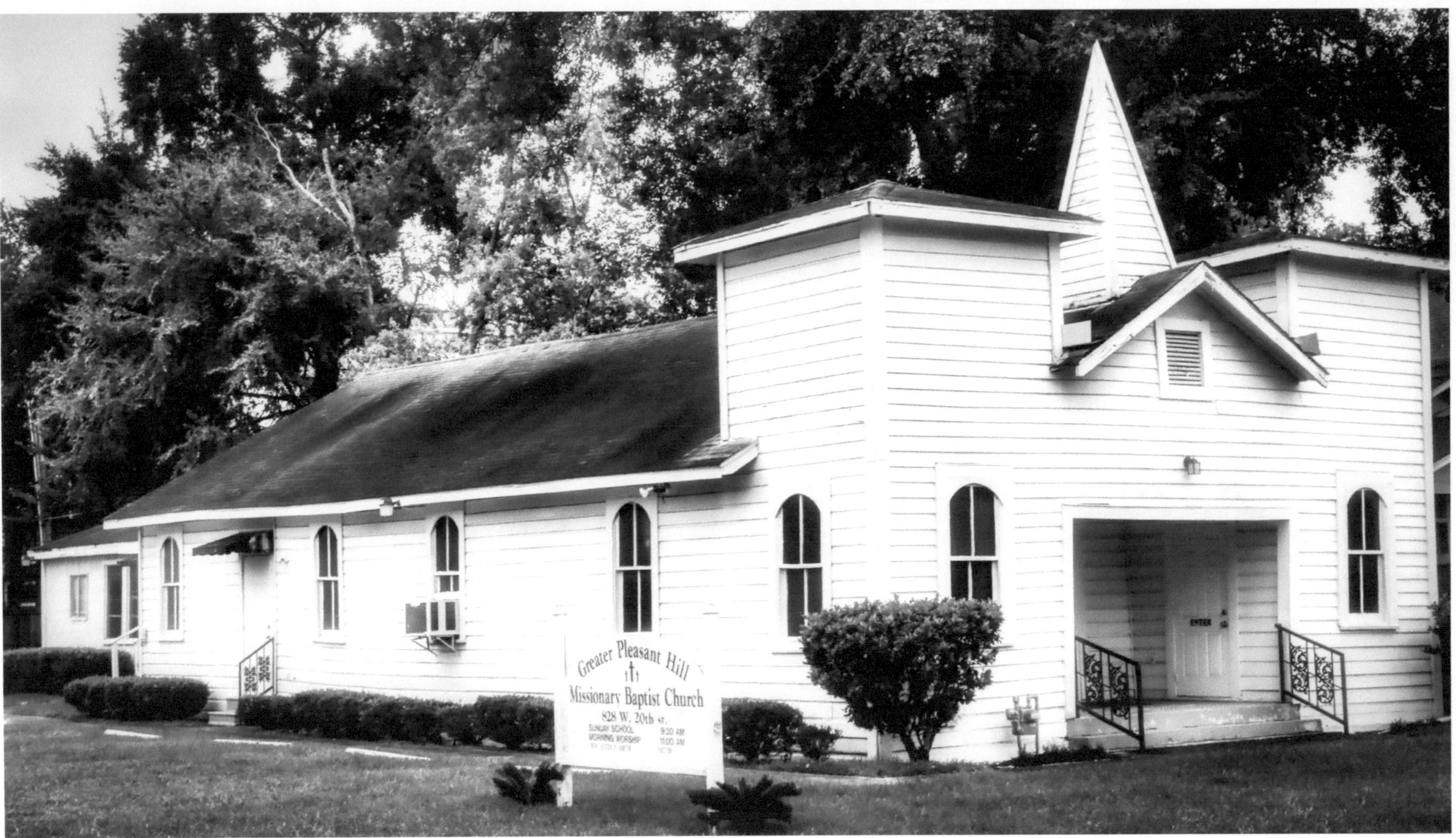

WHITE WOODEN CHURCH

AMOS 5 – (NRSV)

24 But let justice roll down like waters,
and righteousness like an ever-flowing stream.

In all our recollections
In this memory of light
In these eternal moments
Held gently in graciousness
No one may measure
In this sanctuary of faith
In every doubtful turning
Of time's veiled wheel
Chronicles concealed among
Fathomless ageless tales
Passed down through ages
In hope that winter ends
Warming spirits frozen
Motionless in ordinary time
A masquerade that marks
Injustice where such agony
Is held obscurely in hand
Where hesitant history
Is dispelled and mended
Seeing clearly whom they are
Whom they have always been
A people of faith arising
From countless silhouettes
In bereavement and death
And tyrannies borne
By their forebearers
Whose heritage and names
Were abandoned and stolen
In births before and beyond

In stark cruelty imprinted
Upon a people now honored
Within their known stories
We cannot know their pain
Stretched across the centuries
Or oppression endured
Their experience of coercion
We witness with wonder
A gracious radiance glowing
Drawn from their countenance
In this undying brilliance
In these prayers and beneficence
Spoken and unspoken for now
In this light and future memory
The death of grief arrives
Justice proven to transform
Where torments are reconciled
In the strength and sagas
Their ancestors faithfully held
And knew so intimately
So perfectly apprised
Resting in this realization
A people and nation ascend
With burning pride through
Compassion and forgiveness
In this vision they share
Saying to the generations
And to every kind – We rise
We rise – We rise together

GREATER PLEASANT HILL MISSIONARY BAPTIST CHURCH

Houston, Texas – Greater Heights Neighborhood

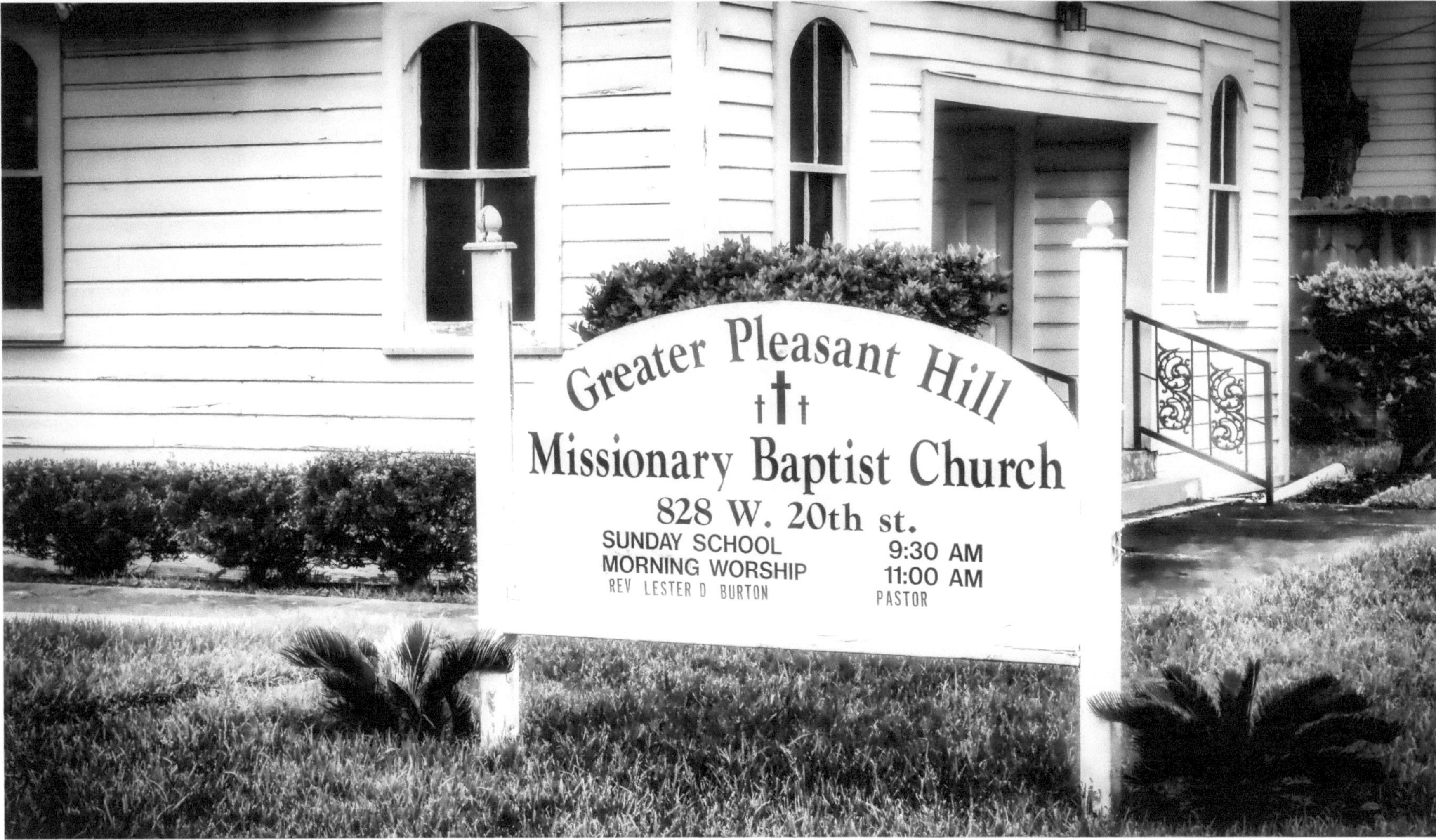

A SEASON OF SORROW

PSALM 31 *In te, Domine, speravi*

1 In you, O Lord, have I taken refuge;
let me never be put to shame;
deliver me in your righteousness.
2 Incline your ear to me;
make haste to deliver me.

In our deepest grief
Earth's fairness fades
And removes itself
From all suffering
Within the world
Becoming a season of sorrow
Where impassive signs
And forebodings
Begin to reign as
We fail to remember
Whom we are
Our brightness gone
Our gardens longing
For heaven's light reflected
Once in a decency lived
In this darkness
We witness our death
Through a single loss
Amid the hardness of life
We do not know how to live

Among the dead
In the anguish
Of our complacency
Remorse haunts us
An illusion steals
Our breath away
In our inability to breathe
In such rigidity
And fear we lose
The point of living
As if it too has moved
Elsewhere and is lost
While heaven bears witness
Watch now – we are being
Transformed through
A deeper memory at work
Within the world
At a point which comes
Much later – when a season
Of hope restores the light

LIVE OAK FRIENDS MEETING

Houston Heights, Texas

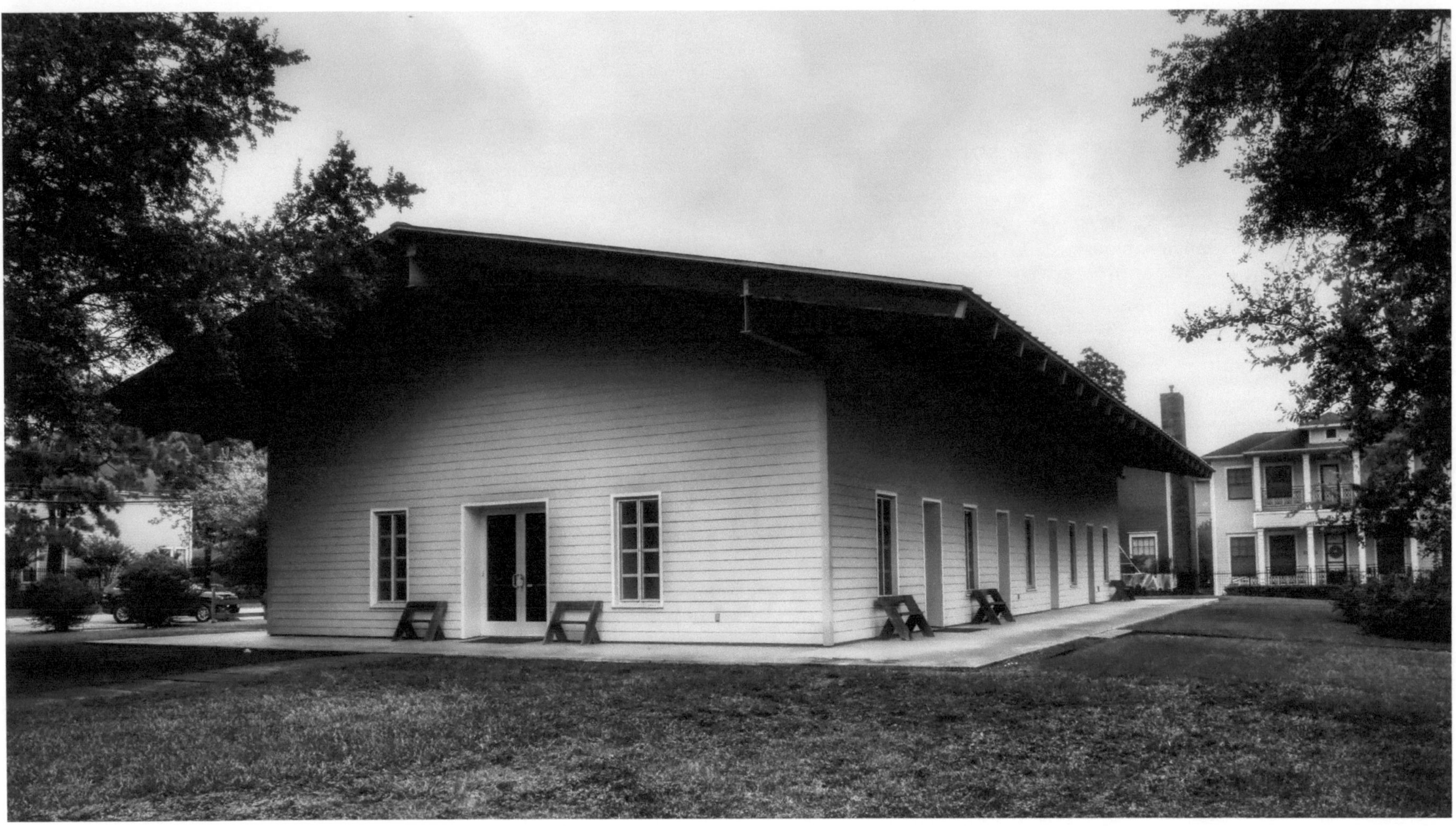

A QUAKER PRAYER

PSALM 27 Dominus illuminatio
1 The Lord is my light and my salvation;
whom then shall I fear?

Let us pray in stillness
In silence — in sacred wonder
as the Friends do

Entering into this place
of holiness by turning thy
mind towards the light

Sit quietly in silence and in strength
while thee wait upon the Lord
with a single heart and eye

A single vision filling thy body with light
Let no other be present but the Lord
Whose spirit waits for thy company

For God is spirit and truth
And in spirit thou may worship
The Lord — waiting in the light

Then let the next person enter
Into this same place
With utter simplicity

Simplicity of heart turn
In thy mind as thee will
Turn in to the light

Let thy heart and self be emptied
Waiting in thy spirit — in the spirit
That quiets all mortal flesh

Where the oneness of God is found
Letting all mortal flesh keep silent
In the stillness of thee God

Come nearer to thy Lord
Then words may lead thee
To know and simply

The goodness of God
Let this tranquility become
An oblation to the Word

A divine first step beyond
all emptiness — empty of
emptiness

Where the oneness
Of thou O God
Becomes known

In such silence
Let the Inner Light glow
Received in silence

LIVE OAK FRIENDS MEETING

Houston Heights, Texas

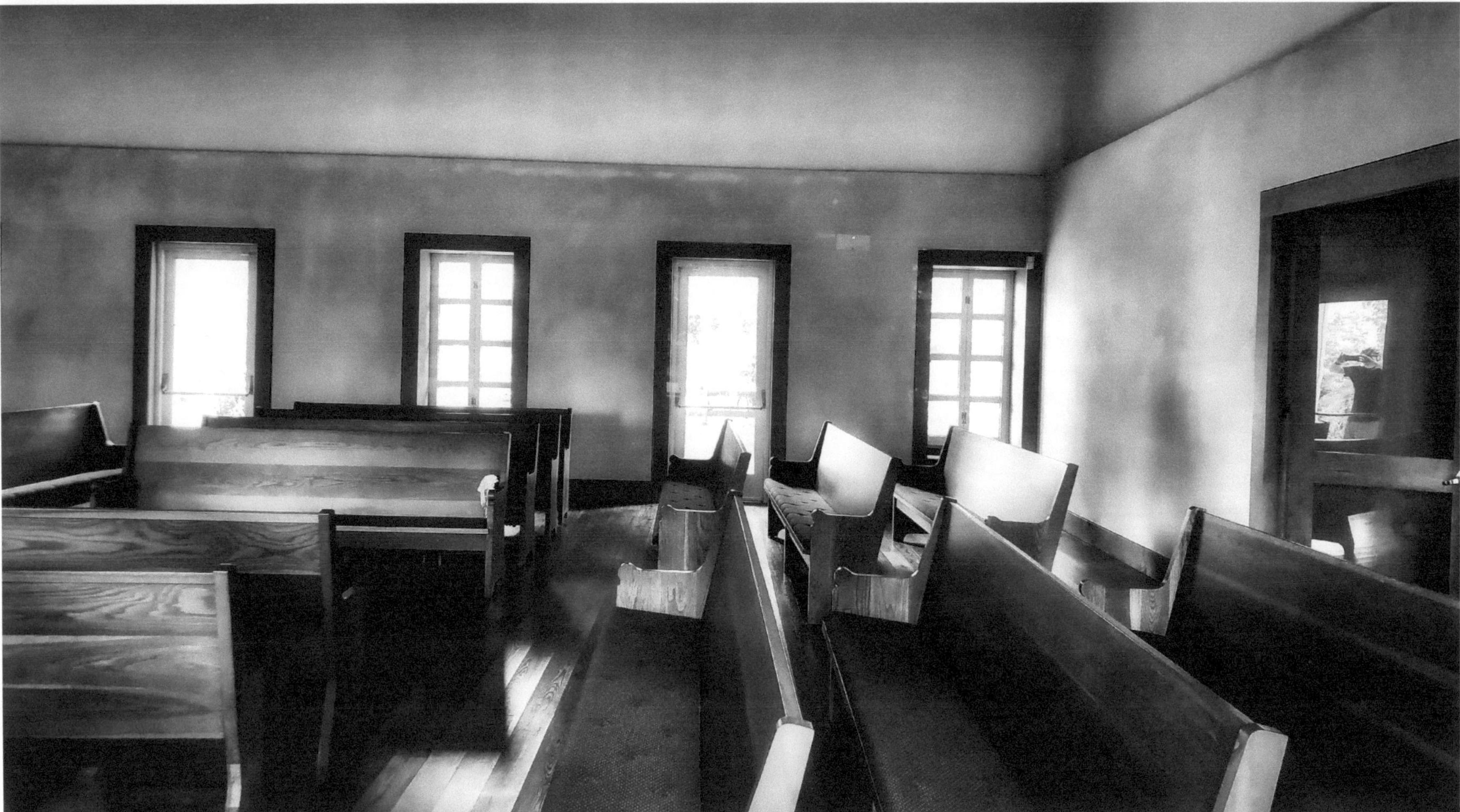

LIVE OAK FRIENDS MEETING

MATTHEW 6 – (AKJV)

22 The light of the body is the eye: if therefore thine eye be single, thy whole body shall be full of light.

In silent worship spaces
I have met friends once more
And looked upon their faces
In shimmering prayerful light
Where no anticipation exists
Except to wait in silence
Always appearing gradually
As anxious thoughts reflect
The earliest days in spring
After a long arctic winter
Tender with yearnings
We do not always know
Until we embrace this calm
In the absence of dogma and doctrine
When we step away from ancient
Creeds and councils cluttering the mind
The ritual of such reticence becomes
A sacrament of faith and mercy
We cannot and may never name
And yet something unexpected
Arises from the tranquility resting
Between and within us now
On a razor's edge of light
We hold with a gentle hope
Waiting in suspense
Balanced delicately between
Our binary observations
And timid choices
So often obscure now
In dichotomies of false choices
Some easily seen — others impossible
To discern without foresight
It is after all hard work seeing
Within ourselves the possible
Expansion of creation
That what our eyes see
Shapes consciousness as truth
As the world forms itself
From the formless energies
Circling round in a chaos
Of crows shadowing us
As a darker distraction
In my imagination I seek
A remembrance of a time
When I am praying with family
My parents and forbearers
Traveling on before us
Sitting together in stillness
Urging us now toward a clearer
Continuity of thought
And bright actions
Before our own light wanes

LIVE OAK FRIENDS MEETING
Houston Heights, Texas

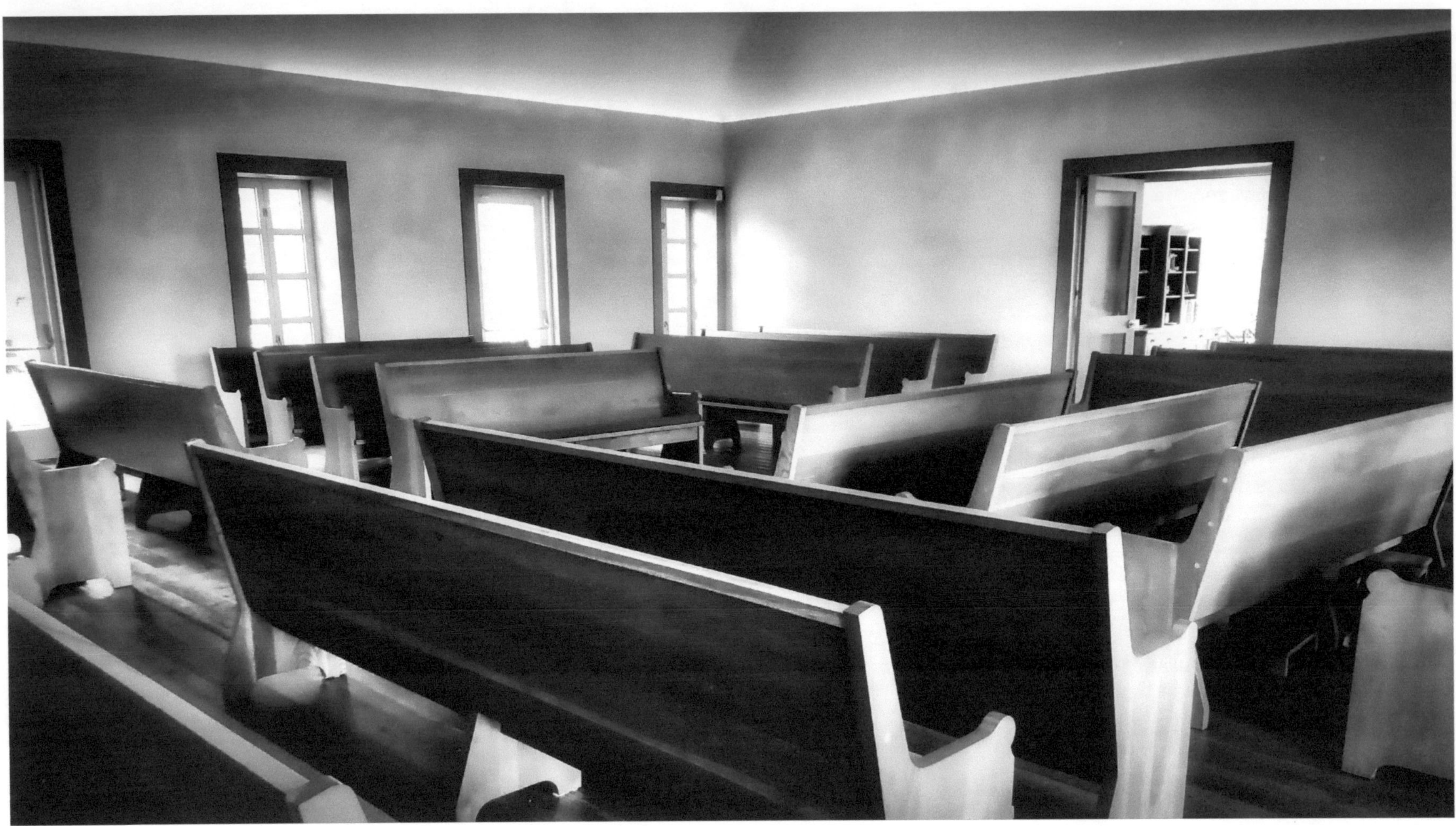

LIVE OAK FRIENDS MEETING

Houston Heights, Texas

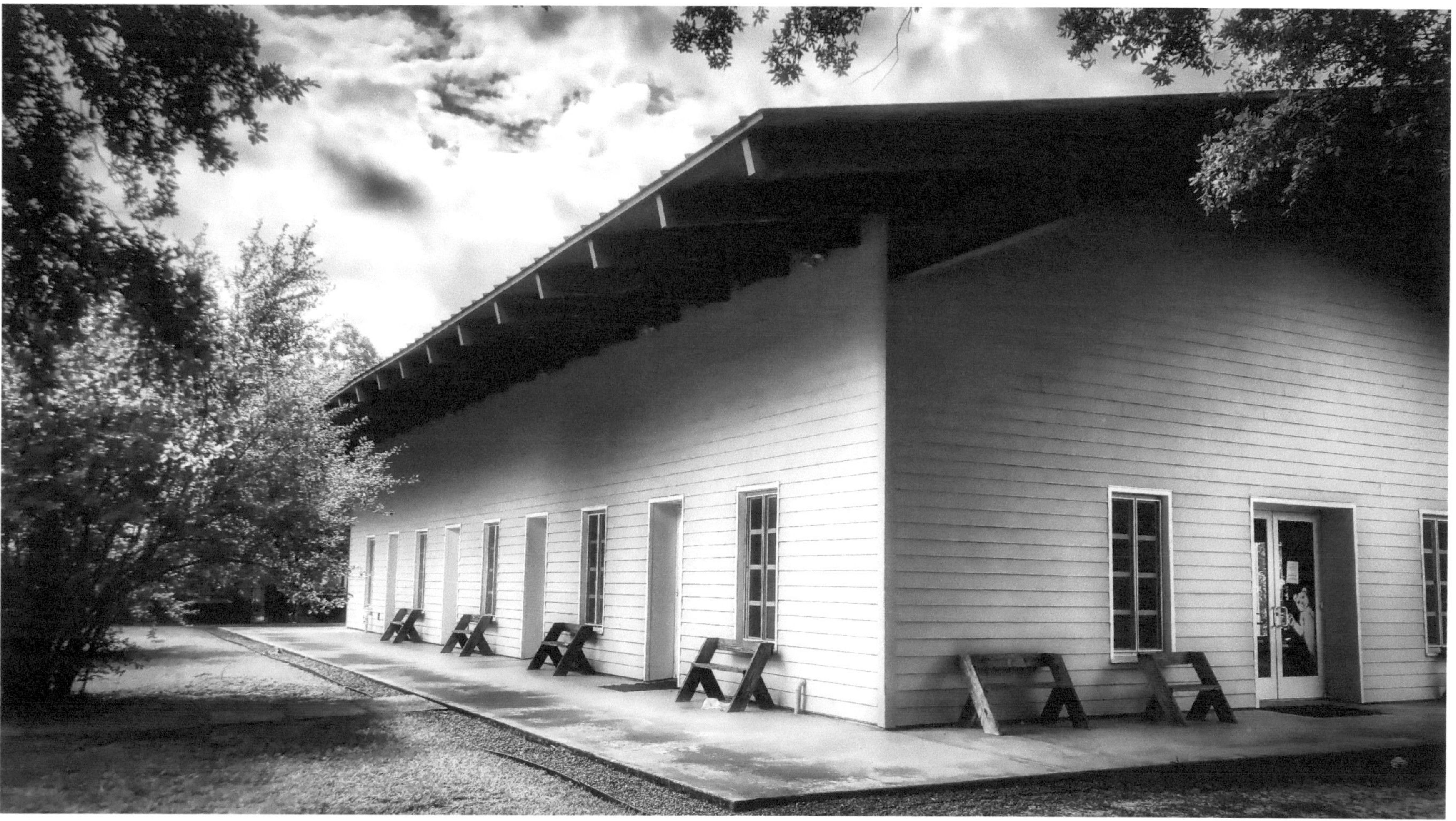

ACKNOWLEDGMENTS & GRATITUDE

I am thankful beyond words for Kevin McGrath, whose friendship and encouragement were selfless. As an esteemed poet, educator, and scholar, Kevin's creative insights were an invaluable resource in working through new possibilities, which arose from our conversations and exchanges.

An especially incredible thanks goes to Elizabeth Cohen for her friendship and care in taking time to review the photographs and poems and to offer her thoughts on the scope and vision of the work in its final stages. And to writer and author, Samme Chittum, who helped me complete the final proof.

Gratitude to Trinity Episcopal Church Midtown Houston, our spiritual community and home for some thirty years, and an inviting place of refuge, worship, and creative partnership with Saint Julian Press.

My humble gratitude must also go out to St. John Lutheran Church in Easton Township, Leavenworth County, Kansas, and Barnard United Methodist Church in Scott Township, Lincoln County, Kansas, for their gracious hospitality and inspiration on this journey.

To Becky and David Claus, close family, who shared their good company and home as a place of refuge and shelter, during these travels.

The final thanks must go to my gracious wife Joanne for all her patience, love, support, and willingness to travel with me on some of the backroads of America and the Southern Great Plains from Kansas to Texas.

NOTES & BIBLIOGRAPHY

1. Front matter epigraph comes from T. S. Eliot's the *Four Quartets – Little Gidding,* fifth movement final verses.
2. A *Pilgrimage of Churches* is divided into geographic regions, with a psalm used as an epigraph to open each one. The Smoky Hills of Kansas flow through the central Great Plains of North America from north-central Kansas and up into southern Nebraska. The psalms used come from *The Psalter* in *The Book of Common Prayer* according to the uses of The Episcopal Church – Church Publishing Incorporated, New York.
3. Pages 2–3: "In This Holy House" was inspired by the United Methodist Church in Beverly, Kansas.
4. Pages 4–7: The poems found here were inspired by what was once Vesper Presbyterian Church in Vesper, Kansas.
5. Pages 8–9: The poem "Generations" and several photographs were inspired by Denmark Lutheran Church in Denmark, Lincoln County, Kansas.
6. Pages 10–1: The poem "God of Abraham" was inspired by the United Methodist Church in Waldo, Kansas.
7. Pages 12–3: The poem "Paradise Creek" was inspired by the UMC and Presbyterian Church in Natoma, Kansas.
8. Pages 14–5: "Solomon River Waterfall" was inspired by the river and falls that runs through the town and municipality of Minneapolis, Ottawa County, Kansas.
9. Pages 16–19: The poems "New Jerusalem" and "Holy Altar" were inspired by the First Methodist Church in Barnard, Kansas. Family lore identifies my paternal great-grandfather as one of the key builders and architects of the church. His father-in-law, my second great-grandfather, was one of the clergy who served the church and a Methodist Circuit Rider in the region. "New Jerusalem" as an allusion draws inspiration from *The Book of Common Prayer* – Pastoral Offices and Sacramental Rites & Services of the Episcopal Church.
10. Pages 20–21: The poem "Union Pacific Train Depot" was inspired by an abandoned railroad line depot in Simpson, Kansas.
11. Pages 22–23: "Nicodemus Rises" was inspired by the African Methodist Episcopal Church in Nicodemus, Kansas, where the United States National Park Services run the Nicodemus National Historic Site. This historic site conserves, safeguards and interprets the one remaining western town established by African Americans during the Reconstruction Period following the American Civil War.
12. Pages 24–27: "Sacred Space" – Images of St. Joseph Catholic Church in Damar, Rooks County, Kansas, and the United Methodist Church community in Agra, Phillips County, Kansas, inspired this poem.
13. Pages 28–30: "Beyond Midwinter Spring" was inspired by the United States Center Chapel and countryside in Lebanon, Kansas.
14. Pages 31: This John Deere photograph is emblematic of America's Great Plains farming and rural communities.
15. Page 33: Psalm 24, *The Psalter* in *The Book of Common Prayer,* opens the photographs and poems in this section, the "Glacial Hills of Kansas" located in the northeastern region of the state.
16. Pages 34–39: "St. John Lutheran" is the church where my maternal grandparents were married in 1920, and my parents in 1948. In 1880, my second-great-grandfather was one of the founding members and trustees of the church. "Family Homestead" includes a recent photograph and a poem regarding the farm where my maternal grandparents raised their family, and where all their children were born. There is a wedding photo from the marriage of Edna Katarina Meinert to Robert Paul Starbuck, on September 5, 1948, at St. John Lutheran Church, Easton Township, Kansas. St. John Lutheran Church and my grandparents homestead and farm were a place of refuge, play, and extended family unity my siblings and cousins knew well since the earliest days of our childhood.

17. Page 40–41: "Sanctuary Lamp" was inspired by St. Paul's Episcopal Church, Leavenworth, Kansas. The words in this poem and meditation are an allusion to and a variation of poetic verses originally written by Queen Elizabeth I, when writing an opinion on the Real Presence of Christ in the Eucharist, while imprisoned at Woodstock, England, during the reign of Queen Mary of Scotland.
18. Pages 42–43: "Wisdom Born" was inspired by Baker University Clarice L. Osborne Memorial Chapel, Baldwin City, Kansas.
    Pages 44–47: "An East 2U7X0m
19. er People" was inspired by St. Mary's Catholic Church and St. Thomas Episcopal Church. St. Mary's is located in the small village of St. Benedict, Nemaha County, Kansas, and is as grand as any church or cathedral found in Europe. St. Thomas Episcopal Church is located in Holton, Kansas, their modest chapel is a 19th century prefabricated building that was mail ordered from Sears & Roebuck and shipped by rail. It is a reminder of a time too many of us have forgotten.
20. Pages 45–49: "Alive With Hope" was inspired by Goff United Methodist Church in Goff, Kansas.
21. Pages 50–51: "Silent Stars" was inspired by Wetmore United Methodist Church in Wetmore, Kansas.
22. Pages 52–55: "Marvelous Remembrance" was inspired by memories of my paternal grandfather and the Wetmore Filling Station & Classic Car Museum.
23. Page 57: The Flint Hills of Kansas, opens with Psalm 33 from *The Psalter* in *The Book of Common Prayer.*
24. Pages 58–60: "Olsburg Bell Tower" was inspired by the United Methodist Church in Olsburg, Kansas.
25. Pages 61–63: "Living the Gospel" was inspired by the United Methodist Church in Westmoreland, Pottawatomie County, Kansas.
26. Pages 64–67: "Thanksgiving Eve" was inspired by the quaint United Methodist Church in Oketo, Marshall County, Kansas. The church is only three miles south of the Nebraska border, its population is around 60 people.
27. Pages 68–69: "Standing in this Light" was inspired by the United Methodist Church in Axtell, Marshall County, Kansas.
28. Pages 70–71: "Gather in this Light" was inspired by the United Methodist Church and St. Malachy's Catholic Church in Beattie, Marshall County, Kansas. Photographs of St. Malachy's will one day be included in a companion book of photographs.
29. Pages 72–73: "Entering In" was inspired by the United Methodist Church in Frankfort, Marshall County, Kansas. Frankfort lost thirty-two of its young men during WWII, more per capita than any other town in America; its population is about 700 today.
30. Page 74–75: "The Old Stone Church" was inspired by an old Congregational Church in the countryside close to Maple Hill, Wabaunsee County, Kansas. The church rests in the Flint Hills, and is no longer active, except on special occasions when families return to honor and remember the ancestors who rest there now.
31. Pages: 76–87: The Flint Hills, with photographs from the Tallgrass Prairie National Preserve and scenic views in the area and south of Matfield Green, Chase County, Kansas. The two poems included were inspired by this countryside.
32. Page 89: Houston–Coastal Plains, opens with Psalm 100 from *The Psalter* in *The Book of Common Prayer.*
33. Pages 90–97: Includes four poems and several photographs inspired by Trinity Episcopal Church in Houston, Harris County, Texas. The poems include "Thanksgiving Praises," "Trinity Acolytes," "Hallelujahs," and "Upon this Eve."
34. Pages 98–101: Two poems, "White Wooden Church," and "A Season of Sorrow," were inspired by Greater Pleasant Hill Missionary Baptist Church in the Greater Heights Neighborhood of Houston, Harris County, Texas. The church appears to be built in the early 20th century.
35. Pages 102–107: Two poems, "A Quaker Prayer," and "Live Oaks Friends Meeting," and were inspired by the Live Oaks Friends Meeting House, Religious Society of Friends, in Houston, Harris County, Texas. The meeting house is well known for its *One Accord Skyspace*, designed by its membership who worked in a creative partnership with artist James Turrell, and architect Leslie K. Elin. These poems also invoke an allusion to words first written by Alexander Parker in 1660, taken from *Quaker faith & practice, Fifth edition* – Religious Society of Friends (Quakers) in Britain.

ABOUT THE AUTHOR

RON STARBUCK is the Publisher/CEO/Editor of Saint Julian Press, a poet/writer and photographer, an Episcopalian, and author of *There Is Something About Being An Episcopalian*, *When Angels Are Born*, *Wheels Turning Inward*, and now *A Pilgrimage of Churches*, four rich collections of poetry following a poet's mythic and spiritual journey that aligns easily with the paths of many contemplative traditions.

Ron has been deeply engaged in an Interfaith-Buddhist-Christian dialogue for many years, and holds a lifelong interest in literature, poetry, Christian mysticism, comparative literature and religion, theology, and various forms of contemplative practice.

He has been a contributing writer for *Parabola Magazine*. And has had poems and essays published in *Tiferet: A Journal of Spiritual Literature*, an interview and poem in *The Criterion: An Online International Journal in English*, *The Enchanting Verses Literary Review*, *ONE from MillerWords* (Feb. 2016), and *Pirene's Fountain, Volume 7 Issue 15*, from Glass Lyre Press (Oct. 2014), *Levure Littéraire* (France – 2017 & 2018), *La Piccioletta Barca* (Nov. 2019), and *The Tulane Review* (Fall 2019). A collection of his essays, poems, short stories, and audio recordings are available on the Saint Julian Press, Inc. website under Interconnections. Several of Ron's new poetry translations, poems, and prose are also available on the www.academia.edu website.

Forming an independent literary press to work with emerging and established writers and poets, and tendering introductions to the world at large in the framework of an interfaith and cross-cultural literary dialogue has been a long-time dream. Ron is a former Vice President with JP Morgan Chase, and a local government and public sector Information Technology Executive Program Manager.

Type Settings & Fonts:

PERPETUA TILTING MT
GOUDY OLD STYLE – Goudy Old Style
GARAMOND – Garamond

www.ingramcontent.com/pod-product-compliance
Lightning Source LLC
LaVergne TN
LVHW070959110826
845147LV00023B/656